ANNELI RUFUS, a prize-winning journalist, is the author of three critically acclaimed nonfiction books, including *Party of One* and *Magnificent Corpses,* and the coauthor of five, most recently *California Babylon.* She has written hundreds of feature articles for magazines and newspapers worldwide, including *Salon,* the *San Jose Mercury News,* the *Seattle Times,* the *San Francisco Chronicle, Westways, California* magazine, and *Image* magazine. She lives in California.

the farewell chronicles

the

farewell

chronicles

[HOW WE *REALLY* RESPOND TO DEATH]

anneli rufus

MARLOWE & COMPANY
NEW YORK

THE FAREWELL CHRONICLES: *How We Really Respond to Death*
Copyright © 2005 by Anneli Rufus

Published by
Marlowe & Company
An Imprint of Avalon Publishing Group Incorporated
245 West 17th Street • 11th Floor
New York, NY 10011-5300

AVALON
publishing group incorporated

Library of Congress Cataloging-in-Publication Data
Rufus, Anneli S.
The farewell chronicles : how we really respond to death / Anneli Rufus.
p. cm.
ISBN 1-56924-381-6 (pbk.)
1. Death—Psychological aspects. I. Title.
BF789.D4R84 2005
155.9'37—dc22
2005012741

9 8 7 6 5 4 3 2 1

Designed by Pauline Neuwirth, Neuwirth & Associates

Printed in the United States of America

For Mom and Dad

contents

[CONTENTS]

introduction

THEY TELL YOU this: When someone dies, you will feel sad.

They warn you about *sad*. It seems so pure. Painful but clean as fire, the way it looks in movies—crying jags. And so you think you know. Even before you lose someone, you think you know. It has been drummed into your head by sad songs (*last chance . . . last kiss . . . tell Laura I love her*), sad films, fairy tales, *King Lear*. Sympathy cards glimpsed on the drugstore rack—why would you look closer at them, or open them, unless you *had* to?—bear generic greetings, punishingly brief. By these scanty prompts you are prepped in the basics of grief: Grieving for Dummies.

And you trust that when the time comes, you will deal with it. You trust that the time will not come tomorrow, or the next day, or the next. And most likely it won't, because we are lucky enough to live in clean safe antiseptic times when, thanks to modern medicine and other miracles, we stand a good chance of reaching adulthood without having yet lost anyone at all.

But then one day it starts. You lose someone. And then it becomes real. Not a sad movie after which you can walk out of the theater into the sunshine, not a sad song you can switch off, but your life. *Your life in death.* In one instant, that split second in which a heart stops, you are transformed into someone who has lost someone. And whoever you were before—your innocence, those smiles—is gone. It's so *back then*, so yesterday. Without meaning to, you have joined a club. It is a vast worldwide society whose members share no privileges, no solidarity, no secret handshakes, no discounts at Legoland. You are just in. And once you're in, you can't rescind your membership. *You can never get out.* Initiation took you by surprise. It was hellish or muted, and now what? Passing each other on the street, sitting side by side on the subway, members of this club do not know each other for what they are, and don't even look up.

You're in a club—a cruel club, because you belong yet you're on your own.

WHEN THAT DAY came, you told yourself: *And now I must be sad.*

And, chances are, you were.

Sadder, quite likely, than you ever could have dreamed. You had no clue how bad it could be, how you could feel stabbed straight through the eyes, flayed in the wind, drowned in gelatin. It lasts.

But that is sorrow. And while you never dreamed that it could feel so bad, I'll say this much for sorrow: *At least you expected it.*

WHAT YOU DID not expect, and what the sad songs never hint about, is all those other ways you feel when someone dies. Weird, messy, nasty, sticky, scary reactions that slop over the rim of sorrow, or infiltrate it, or flavor it, or poison it, or take its place.

You were not warned. You were not taught. No one ever sat you down and told you: Some deaths, someday, will make you sigh with bittersweet relief. Others will make you think you caused them. You will say, *It's my fault.* Sometimes regret will spin you in an everlasting lonely oxygenless orbit. No one ever sat you down and said: Some deaths will horrify you. Grisly things no one should see you will never be able to forget. Some deaths will make you think you hate the dead one, while others will make you think you hate yourself. Still others will make you think you hate everyone alive. No one sat you down and said: Hark. Mind what you do. Words left unspoken in life cannot be said to the dead nor can what has been said be taken back. There *are* such things as never and forever and too late. No one warned you about wouldhave couldhave shouldhave, singsonging in your head. No one told you to picture yourself greedy, scrambling for the leavings of the dead. They never said some deaths would shame you. Some would make you selfish. No one ever warned you that some deaths would silence you, as if you had come to live at the bottom of a well.

THEY NEVER SAID that death does funny things to love, and love does funny things to death. They never warned you that death is a brutal and relentless thresher separating those you loved from those you thought you loved or those you thought you ought to love and those you feigned loving on purpose or because you did not know what else to do. They never said some deaths would set you free. They never said some deaths would make you glad. They never said some deaths would make you feel nothing at all.

. . .

THEY NEVER TOLD you the most crucial fact of all:

There is no right way to react to death and no wrong way. Neither a good way nor a bad.

There is no template into which you, by virtue of having lost someone, must fit yourself. No system by which to measure the perfect mourner. No ideal. No Q&A in which you check boxes and calculate your score. *Am I a proper mourner?* There are sad-song, sympathy-card myths. Then there is life. And you.

And no two mourners mourn alike. No two lives are alike, nor are any two deaths: beyond the clinical facts, every death is a *Rashomon*. Each witness escapes with a different tale to tell.

Because you were not trained in grief, never researched it in your happy days—because you arrive in its midst naive—its nasty sticky messy side comes as a shock. You imagine your outlook to be aberrant and anomalous, thus unacceptable. You blame yourself. Someone has died and you call yourself a freak. Unfaithful. Unholy. Unfilial. Unfeeling. Infantile. Cold. Cruel. Selfish. Insane.

You've lost someone, and you feel like a criminal.

BUT YOU TELL no one, because you suspect that no one could ever possibly understand these inappropriate feelings of yours. You suspect that no one else ever felt this way. What else can it be but the sick fruits of a twisted mind? Because, face it, whoever heard of any dirges written specially for glad or greedy mourners? Have you ever seen a headstone on which was engraved, YOU ARE GONE, YET I CANNOT CRY?

A death is shocking. Witnessing a death will put you in a

state of shock. Even if you did not love him or her who died, the principle of death alone still gets you. The concept, the idea of a corpse and what happens to it, and where the soul goes. Even if you did not love or even like (or hardly knew) the one who died, you cannot help but think, *I might be next.* And you reel. Stagger. Pretending that you can handle it only intensifies the shock. And so, for that matter, does love. Who could possibly handle it? You get up on the morning of the funeral and put on decent clothes and walk around embracing well-wishers with an expression of gratitude. Then back at work your colleagues say, *So sorry,* and you nod and thank them for their sympathy. You walk down the street looking blank. You are not handling it at all.

Our ancestors could not afford to hide from death. It sought them everywhere—in wars, plagues, natural disasters, child-birth, childhood, old age at twenty or thirty. Our ancestors watched each other drop like flies. Then they cleaned and dressed their own dead for the grave or tomb or pyre. They sat up all night, keeping vigil, with corpses. They knew the touch of newly dead flesh, five days' dead flesh, ash or bone. Displaying grief in public was not a matter of choice for them: they turned it into a spectacle. Mourners slashed their own flesh with rocks and sticks. Some knocked out their own teeth. Some remained silent for a year. Some flung themselves into the pit or pyre.

Those days are gone. Death keeps its distance from our anti-septic lives. We have even refined our word for it. These days we say *pass* instead of *die.* It sounds softer, with upbeat connotations: *Pass me the ball. A free pass. He passed the test!* In word and deed, we keep our sorrow soft. And sorrow, within limits, will shock no one, horrify no one, even these days. Cry and the world cries with you—at least a bit, at least for a while. But cry too loudly or too long, or not at all, or mixed with weirder stuff, and observers will scrutinize you, diagnose you, exhort you to pull yourself together, get on with it, get a life.

Our safe clean surroundings cloak a conspiracy of silence. We smile, scared of ourselves, scared of death but scared even of being scared. *I'm fine*, we lie. We smile, hoping the nausea will go away. We smile, praying that no one can tell how we really feel. Denying ourselves, exiling ourselves, we smile.

This is not a book about sorrow per se. It pokes into sorrow and past sorrow and through sorrow and under sorrow into the nasty weird stickiness that comes after we lose someone and which we might as well admit, we might as well embrace— because it is ours after all.

BUT WHO AM I? A death expert? No, only a member of the club.

By the time I was thirty and my dad died of a stroke, I had already lost more acquaintances than most young moderns lose in a whole lifetime. I was unusual, like some kind of vortex. The first was my babysitter, twelve-year-old Cecile with the fluffy blonde hair and red clam-digger pants and ladybug earrings, who tucked me into bed with my stuffed corduroy clown. Cecile was on vacation when a boulder tumbled down a mountainside and crushed her. The next was Troy Armitage from down the block, run over while riding his ten-speed in the street. Kids gathered to watch city workers spray the asphalt with a high-test hose. In fifth grade, Oscar Salazar fell off a roof. In sixth grade, Terence Coons whom everyone called Terry-dactyl was visiting his best friend who took a gun from a drawer and said, *It belongs to my dad. He never keeps it loaded*, pointed it and shot. The next year, doing backflips in gym class, Lauren Boehm collapsed: quiet Lauren, with her two-tone platform shoes: her heart was weak, and no one knew. Eighth grade was a reprieve, but then in ninth grade, Patrick Ostrovich was riding to the beach in a VW that slammed into a van. He had just been voted Best Looking in our class, Patrick with his sun-streaked hair and slate-blue eyes. That was the way we learned, in science class, the term *brain-dead*. Also that year, Joe Pirelli who flirted with my best friend Jeannette and borrowed her ballpoint pens but never gave them back: another day, another drawer, another gun. The choir at his funeral sang Ambrosia's hit "Holdin' On to Yesterday." Chris Gaines moved away to Texas and drowned in a lake. That summer, my mother had a friend, Millie, whose nine-year-old son had stomach cancer. A friend of my father's walked into a lab at work that year without realizing that a container of toxic chemicals had begun to leak; he walked out and dropped dead at his desk.

That year was like a massacre. Then came the next.

I thought of death more than most young girls do, not because I longed for it but because it was everywhere: at school and at the Munich Olympics and in our tract whose ranch-style houses were the pinks and greens and whites of after-dinner mints. The night my boyfriend took me home to meet his family, I jabbered about murderers. *This one guy in Wisconsin flayed his victims and made vests out of their skins!* I took a Mystic Mint from the platter as Todd's father glanced up from the football game. *He made their lungs into stews!*

I did not long for death, but I thought about it all the time because it seemed to make no sense. I thought that if I kept thinking about it I might understand it, or accept it. Or escape it.

WHEN MY DAD died, death took on a new dimension. It slipped out of the abstract, the vicarious, and the baroque and into the glint of intravenous tubes. My shoes smelled of hospital. So *this* is how death feels when it takes not a classmate but the man who cuddled you and yelled at you in public, who taught you how to read and mix concrete and use a microscope.

And it was in that aftermath—as his last pre-stroke word kept roaring in my head: it was *Nintendo*—that I realized that what I felt was not pure sorrow at all. It was other things about which I could not tell my mother or anyone else. Sure, I was sad, but I thought: am I sad enough? And if I did miss him, why did I keep rehashing the way he used to storm into my room and yell, *You fucking slob,* his hard backhand, his slip-on shoes stomping enraged, *Goddamn goddamn,* his laughter as he eavesdropped on my dance lesson: *You look like you gotta go pee!* I thought too of his tanned perfect fingers working a power tool, a slide rule, designing satellites for the U.S. government. His eyes sliding shut as he listened to Grofé's *Grand Canyon Suite.* The gleam of his teeth that looked just like my teeth; the way we could walk together on the beach for hours without having to speak. Why did I invoke the monster in him? Why, if I loved him? *Did* I love him?

He used to sing *You are my sunshine*. At my wedding, he wore a necktie printed with crossed guns marked HIS and HERS. One of the last times I saw him, he seized my arm in a crosswalk and screamed, *Goddamn you*.

Sitting there in my hospitaly shoes, I tried to be the perfect little grieving girl. As if someone would see me and say, *Good*. As if this were another portion of the SAT. As if.

SIX YEARS LATER, on the night of our high school reunion, my best friend Jeannette and I wore party dresses—hers light, mine dark, as always. Crossing the hotel lobby, we could see Mylar balloons trailing green ribbons—our class color—in the ballroom. Music from our graduation year pumped through the speakers. Women were shouting like teenage girls. *Hiiii!*

In the corridor stood an easel, on which was a posterboard printed with the words IN MEMORIAM. It was a list of all our classmates who had died.

We already knew about some of them. The suicides: the guitarist who shot himself, the mother of four who drove off a cliff into the sea. The former tennis star killed in a carjacking. Others surprised us. *Him? But how? Was she the one who wore the same shirt every day?* The list gave only names, not dates or reasons.

Jeannette stamped her foot and swore.

That stupid shit.

Derek was second from last on the list.

HE WAS OUR shadow for two years. Everywhere we went, he came, too.

Jeannette met him in the quad. She liked him right away—but not *like that*. He was gay. He liked her, too, called her his best friend, which was weird because she was *my* best friend. And so we were three. He made fun of me. My feet. My ears. My virginity: he loved to talk to girls about their sex lives, so Jeannette—of course she did—told Derek in that teenage way, rocking on sneakered heels, *Roo has never been popped!* The things he said. I should have gone away or punched him out, but never. Only when Jeannette and I left for our separate universities could I be certain never to see him again. *They* stayed in touch. He told Jeannette about the clubs in Hollywood. The guys. She told him to be safe. He told her sure, but sometimes guys get high and stuff happens so fast. She said, *Be safe*. At first it was a joke, but then they fought. *Reckless*, spat Jeannette. *Mind your own business, bitch*, he said and hung up. She never called back. And now this.

I warned that stupid shit.

The crowd was flowing through the doorway and pulling us in. Couples jived on the dance floor, ex-cheerleaders and sharp-suited guys with double chins.

Our ex-classmate Teresa wandered up to us.

You saw that about Derek, she said. Her shoulders sagged. *He died in my arms.* When he got really sick, she let him stay in her apartment. He had sores and did not want the world to see. When we were still in school, Derek was not nice to Teresa, either, but the difference between her and me was that she never knew when he was being mean.

He had a vision at the end, she said, sipping vodka and Coke. She had a new tattoo. She narrowed her eyes at Jeannette. *He said some-one was waving to him from the window of a Porsche and it was you.*

He was a gifted acrobat and a devoted son and he was dead so young and that was sad.

Stupid shit. Jeannette speared a broiled shrimp. *What a completely stupid and unnecessary way to die.* Her eyes were red and wet but her jaw jerked from side to side. Its sinews made a popping sound, the way they always did when she was mad.

Teresa turned her plate around as if it were a wheel. *I mean, that's funny, isn't it?* She flashed a smile at Jeannette that was not a smile. *You of all people. In his last vision.*

A new song started, and I feigned being absorbed in it, the way I used to in the car or on the beach, so that no one would pay me any mind. *That ditz. She loves her rock and roll.* Because no way should Jeannette and Teresa see, no way should anyone, what I was thinking. Yes, he was a gifted acrobat a gifted acrobat a gifted acrobat and so nice to his mom his mom his mom. And such a bastard to me—he knew, he was well aware, he knew exactly what he was doing and saying back then and to whom. He knew. And now he could not do that anymore. If I stared hard enough into the disco lights, no one could see me smile.

And we were all together but apart.

HOW COULD OUR responses to death *not* be messy? Death is about relationships. Death is about the future and the past. Death is a mystery. We fear our own. It mocks us, that frontier you cannot cross with any hope of coming back. You contemplate the cusp, and don't know what to do. And that darkness inside you, that murk which you find shocking and unspeakable, is part of the story, is what you take away. And even at its worst, you are richer for it.

Sorrow is not enough. It is not all.

Someone dies and goes away. Yet never goes away.

It stops. It never stops.

the farewell chronicles

I.

evasion

When I moved into the Alsace Arms, its six stucco stories rising from a corner like a buttercream-frosted cake, its manager was an eighty-four-year-old man named Mr. Kalb. He had moved into his second-floor studio fifty years before, when the building was new. Each apartment boasted curved cathedral windows, an arched niche cut into the wall for a phone, and a built-in buffet with glass doors. The Alsace Arms was rent-controlled, so half of its occupants were students and the other half were elderly. A daily visit to Campus Liquor & Snack across the street was the only daily sortie for some of the older tenants: you saw them trundling across the street in rain bonnets and cardigans, carrying mesh shopping bags.

Every month a get-together was held in the lobby, with its white Ionian columns and large mirrors. That is where I met the blind student who wore only blue and white so as never to clash, though I wondered how he *knew* his clothes were blue and white. Did a sighted person shop for him, and how could he trust that person? Or did he shop by himself, trusting the clerks? It would certainly be easy to sell him a green shirt as a joke. Another tenant was a university junior who worked as a sexual surrogate: someone for shy and nervous men to practice with. She looked like Stevie Nicks and I imagined her stroking their hair, speaking to them gently about breath control and hygiene. And I heard from yet another tenant that the white-haired lady in tweed and linen had lost the love of her life at the Battle of the Somme: *Iris Beane promised herself to a boy*, said her neighbor who collected saucers. *But he never came back. So she lives loving his memory. Happened to lots of girls*, the neighbor said.

The man whose apartment was directly over mine was writing a mystery novel about a killer who poisoned women with cyanide. *It smells of almonds!* he would say and sniff the air. Another tenant was a French lady who went outside before dawn with scissors and a bag and snipped flowers from other people's front yards. She rushed back with armloads of lilies and roses.

MR. KALB MOVED into a nursing home and his apartment stood empty for only a day before the new manager arrived. The son of Mrs. Ayyad on the sixth floor, he was thirty-two and, the neighbors said, had left a job in the Manhattan theater scene but wanted to be near his mother, who brewed coffee the Egyptian way and was a hunchback.

Before I saw him, I saw the signs he posted around the lobby. *Wipe your feet on mat don't track mud on hall carpit! Keep garage door SHUT open doors attract theives thank you! Radiators will be repaired soon bare with me!* He signed each one *Jihad*. That was his name.

Jihad. At the time the word held no meaning for me. He later had to tell me what it meant and how ridiculous a name it was for him. His late father had been an Egyptian diplomat.

Jihad brought empanadas to that next get-together: beef in flaky pastry pockets. They were delicious. *I love to cook!* he yelled waving his arms, which made him look even leaner in yellow jeans and a striped satin blouson.

He asked us all to drop in anytime and visit him. Being the manager meant sitting in his flat all day in case a tenant or the landlords needed him. The landlords were a pair of brothers who lived miles away and also owned a Laundromat and a Korean restaurant. Jihad grew bored easily. *Why read, if it's not something about me? There's lots been written about me, girlfriend.* He liked to gossip about the other tenants. Gina, the sexual surrogate: *Pretty, but that perm—oh, shoot me!*

Lying back on his red velvet couch, he exhaled through long nostrils, chain-smoking Gauloises. The air between us was hazy, coils of smoke unspooling on the ceiling. A coffee table held a clown-shaped ashtray and a peacock feather in a Cointreau bottle.

Under the coffee table were stacks of photo albums. *Here I am,* he would say, pushing an open album onto my lap, pointing at a picture, *dressed to kill.* In New York he had not been in the theater actually. He was a cross-dresser who wore upswept hairstyles that showed off his smooth apricot shoulders. He said a series of married businessmen had called him Cinnamon and paid his rent. *When I walked into a place, I looked like* this, Jihad would say and strike a haughty pose. *And everyone else looked like* this. He mimed men ogling, slack-jawed.

He had started cross-dressing at sixteen but by thirty he had begun to wrinkle. Younger guys were just more popular. He started wearing his hair long and straight to hide the creases in his neck and changed from strappy tops to long-sleeved shirts to hide the blotches on his arms and back. He was about to go on food stamps when his mother told him Mr. Kalb was leaving.

Milk in your tea? You should skip the sugar, he said now, lifting the creamer to my cup, his lips and tongue shaping the smoke from his Gauloise into short syncopated puffs, like smoke signals in a cartoon. He scried my face. *No sugar for you, girlfriend.*

He liked having me around. He turned the clock to face the wall so that I never could say it was time to leave. He liked hearing himself talk. *Change your name,* he would say, *tomorrow—to Silk.*

HE MISSED HIS New York friends, he missed culture. In the lobby he hung pictures of artworks cut from magazines. He was not good at fixing things. He drove screws into walls using a hammer. He repaired peeling linoleum with Scotch tape. For plumbing and electrical repairs, he walked up to Telegraph Avenue and asked the beggars there whether any of them were handy. He would bring them back and they would use Mr. Kalb's tools, then they would bathe in Jihad's tub and sleep on his couch. Before cleaning the tub he liked to show me the black rings they left around it.

He was filthy! But pink as a baby when he washed.

ONE DAY I arrived to find him scribbling on a sheet of graph paper.

I've just finished my blueprint, he said with a smile, waving it at me. It was a design for a roof spa on top of the Alsace Arms, with palm trees and a pool. It would require tearing a hole through the sixth-floor ceiling for the pool, and installing stairs to the roof. *Or,* he said, *we could have a rope ladder.*

He faxed the blueprint to the landlords. They turned him down.

He drew up another plan, this time with shuffleboard and cabanas and a waterfall that poured down the side of a full-service bar complete with bartender. The Kims called Jihad to say that tenants were forbidden to go onto the roof, it was in violation of city codes.

He drew more blueprints. He just stopped sending them anywhere.

One day we were in his apartment when he looked around sharply and whispered, *That bitch Iris is listening to us.* Iris Beane lived next door.

She listens through the air vents.

She does not, I said.

How would you know? He punched his knees. *I think she tapes me with a tape recorder.*

He also stopped speaking to the blind guy, who Jihad said had laughed at him in the laundry room.

I STARTED FINDING excuses not to visit Jihad anymore. When we ran into each other on the stairs I would act as if I were late for an appointment. He would smile faintly. One night he grinned and gave a double thumbs-up.

Had a checkup today, he said. *The doctor says I'm fine!*

That's great, I said.

Come for a cup of tea?

Sorry, I said. *No time.*

One night I found him in the elevator. He was just standing in there, riding it up and down. Its door opened as I was passing through the lobby.

Is it broken? I said.

No. He beckoned to me and looked around, holding the button that kept the doors open. He was smoking a Gauloise despite his own sign taped up right behind him, which said *No Smoking in Here Thank You!*

I have a problem, Jihad said. *I have been placed under surveillance.*

By whom? I said.

Not sure. He looked back and forth. *Iris, maybe. Cameras and microphones are planted all over my flat. And someone must be drugging me, because I feel like shit.*

He let the door slide shut and rode the elevator up.

A FEW DAYS after that, he was mopping the lobby floor. As he worked, he wheezed, and he had a facial sore.

I pretended I didn't know what that meant but I knew.

A few days after that I saw him standing on the curb out front with a valise. It was a warm day but he was wearing layers of sweaters and rubbing his arms. A gauze patch covered the sore.

I called a cab. He pooched his lips, enunciating *cawwwled* the New York way. *I have a ticket to Hawaii.*

[EVASION]

Wow! I said. *How cool!*
My sister in Atlanta bought it for me.
Cool! I said. *Well, see ya.*
Jihad greeted the cab driver with a wave.

HE WAS NOT supposed to come back. He was supposed to die there, in the clinic by the ocean where his sister had booked him a bed.

He was not supposed to come back, but could not stand the slowness of Hawaii, which is why I saw him in the hall again a month later. I saw him from the back, but it was him.

Did I call his name? Did I call, did I visit, did I bring a bag of fruit?

Never.

Another month later a vase of roses picked by the French tenant stood on the mail table alongside a sheet of paper on which were written the words IN MEMORY, and a snapshot of Jihad as a child wearing a shiny party hat.

At the next get-together, Mrs. Ayyad wept. His last week in the hospital was horrible, she said. *Khowreeball.* She said Jihad cried right till the end. *He did not want to say good-bye, that boy!*

He had been taken to the hospital after falling down one day in his flat and being unable to stand back up. He screamed, and Iris Beane called 911.

YOU AVOID THE dying, more than you should.

Even your friends. You make up reasons—*We'd stopped being friends! He went crazy and then we stopped!* The fact that he was going crazy because he was sick, because AIDS sometimes took hold of the brain—you ask yourself, who knew that then?

He just seemed crazy. An unpleasant crazy man, such as everyone avoids. After he became crazy, he was no longer my friend. Thus, somewhat later, when he appeared ill, I was not obliged to look after him or even ask about him because we were no longer friends. So there you have it. Q.E.D.

Excuses such as that are soothing for five minutes.

Then you realize what a skunk you are.

Spending time with the dying is so hard, one of the hardest things. I hardly need to say why—the sadness, the physicality of sickness in its sights and sounds and smells, the way every sentence spoken is a kind of good-bye, back and forth for a day, a week, a year, good-bye, good-bye. The effort of the dying to seem strong and not to bum you out completely, and your effort in return to do the same, plus how much cheer is cheering and how much is too much, how much listen-to-this-fun-thing-that-happened-to-me will make the sick one miserable as he or she compares and contrasts? I hardly need to say. You know, and knowing is why you avoid them.

Bad.

You tell yourself that you have more time, that you will get around to it, pick up the phone but only when the time is right, drop in but never unexpectedly, how rude, only after a call and you *will* call, you will, but only when the time is right. I mean, he isn't going to die *today*.

I could have asked his mother. *How long has Jihad been paranoid?* I could have asked a friend of mine who was a psychotherapist.

Could I have your opinion please? No cure for what he really had of course, but I knew nothing of that then and in the white caldera of his fears I left him all alone. The fears he talked about and the ones he did not. I slipped away on tippytoes, pretending not to know.

And when he was crazy *he was crazy*, a mind bending before my very eyes, and he became a narrative I told. *My crazy manager.* The gothic sound of it. A chronicle, a yarn.

That sore on his lip—please, put two and two together. I could have but I did not, and did not comfort him. Nor say *I know, just rest*. I did not say a word except, *Wow! Cool! Vacation!*

I watched him fissure, and walk a crooked mile. An AIDS death is not an attractive death. Not a slow darling fade such as you find in stories like *Heidi*.

I stayed away out of cowardice. A hard cold panic hissing unattended in a black box in my head. Watching from the staircase is one thing but beyond my comprehension would have been going to his room anymore, talking to someone shaking and breaking right before your eyes like a bottle of cream spoiled and explosive in the sun. Seeing the pus, the blood, the spit which was the syrup of destruction. Digging through prosaic memories, I wondered afterward, when he was dead, my heart racing: *Did he bleed in the empanadas? How many times did we share a cup? Oh God. Oh God.* And all the while imagining hearing him say in crazy diction how it feels to die.

I could have spent an hour each day. I lived in the same building after all. Even an hour a *week*. Later I heard that Léonie, the French tenant, did all his laundry in the last two months and washed his dishes from the meals his mother made. The blind man gave him a blanket.

We are terrified to see flesh putrefying even as it sits talking and eating sandwiches. The young flesh in the act of insurrection, cells turned into mutineers.

We are animals who see the weak one in the herd and sprint, letting it fall behind, letting the lion get it. Sprinting, we dare not turn back and see it lying there, convulsing on the veldt, eyes beseeching the sky.

We run.

Some creatures can suppress this impulse long enough to care: to stop, and—even when the whiff of death is as strong as hairspray—*to sit and stay*. Some creatures can. I am a wildebeest, a halibut.

Visiting the catastrophically ill is technically a mitzvah, a good deed, according to Jewish law, yet you might argue, *What's the point? I mean, be philosophical*—the dying person's going to die, he won't remember after he dies who did his laundry and who did not. He will be *gone*, so what future is there in nurturing a relationship of which one thing is certain: that it has no future? Might as well (you could argue) call it a day right now. What difference do a few weeks or months make? OK, your brother or your best friend is a different story altogether. So different as to not even beg discussion or debate. You know for whom you, no matter where or when, would be there, for whom you would make every minute last. But the rest? Those you like but do not love? It is not a reflex, then, not a force by which you would cross mountains rivers valleys to offer a damp towel or a slice of buttered toast, or your own marrow if someone said please.

The degree to which you like a dying person whom you do not love is not a calculation that feels nice to make. Thus, your excuses: Well, it would be wrong to rob his relatives and closest friends of precious time that *they* can spend with him now, so close to the end! Or come to think of it, I bet he wants to be alone. If I were ill, would I want guests? Of course not! Does he want others to see him groan in pain, puke, have a facial tic or lose control of his bowels or, for that matter, cry? No, he does not! He longs to be alone. How can he make peace with his God if you are sitting there trying to get him to play crazy eights? Avoiding him is an act of conscience, kindness, and grace.

And how well do you even know him anyway? Not well! You first met him a year ago, two years. What were you to him, and what was he to you? Nothing, or nearly so. What was between you was a puff of smoke, a breeze. It was not really friendship. It just happened. You would not have picked each other out from a crowd. And what about that stuff he did that made you mad? The time—*before* he went crazy, OK?—he promised he would be somewhere but never showed. The time he said he would feed your fish when you were away and he forgot. Remember what you said that time, after the fish? (They did not starve to death but almost, you could tell.) Sure you remember what you said. *Screw it, why did I ever call that jerk a friend? He's not my friend, he never was my friend.*

Before the symptoms, that was.

Reflecting on how it was over anyway, you tell yourself how awkward it would be to show up now. (Of course it would not really—he would probably be grateful. But you don't tell yourself that.) You tell yourself his fragile health could not support a visit from an ex-friend who made no secret of having soured on him, back then. Think what the awkwardness would do to his weak heart. Why, your visit could kill him! What would that make you—a murderer?

The mind will believe anything.

AFTER JIHAD DIED, I swore I would not avoid the dying anymore. Not even if I only liked them a little, much less a lot. They needed me—they need whomever can amuse them or divert them or comfort them. They need what they need.

I swore it, hounded by memories of Jihad and picturing, as years went by, the dying person shunned by everyone, sitting sick and alone watching *Dialing for Dollars* or Richard Simmons, the dying person rendered a wallflower, rendered a pariah because the world has so many cowards. In his last hours, what if something you said soothed him through?

Let them leave knowing others cared. Let them leave not loathing themselves.

I told myself.

So one day, ten years after Jihad died, a notice went up on the bulletin board where I worked. It said that our former receptionist, a woman named Daisy who was my mother's age, had just been diagnosed with pancreatic cancer and had been given a few months to live.

Daisy was an ex–*Newsweek* reporter who became our receptionist at sixty-five, just for a kick. And to get access to a health plan, she used to say—as a joke, because Daisy was quick and spry. One morning in our office kitchen, she vaulted onto the counter to rescue a wasp. She became a Zen Buddhist in the 1950s and lived on the temple grounds. She said, Come over for a morning service anytime, and I always said, Sometime. Anytime! she said. Because the great thing about temples is, they always wait. She had beautiful penmanship, all loops and whorls like skaters leave in ice. After my father died, Daisy would always ask me how my mother was. She never met my mother, but still. *Does she have places to go? Does she have friends?* Daisy would ask.

Daisy retired at seventy, but did not look that old. I saw her sometimes at the Y. She always said hello, and that life was serene in her cottage behind the shrine. Then that day—the bulletin board.

It said Daisy was resting at home after surgery, which had shown that she could not be saved. I could have gone right then, that day. I knew exactly where the temple was.

Instead of going, I sent her a card. Not a get-well card, obviously. My dad used to make me write personal greetings inside cards he bought for colleagues whose birthday it was or who were getting married or were ill or had spouses who'd died. I used to try to get out of that chore, tell him it was *his* card, the sentiment would seem fake if it came from me. He made me do it, though, so all those newlyweds and birthday boys and widowers got messages from me, sometimes in rhyme, signed *Dave*.

Writing to Daisy, on the other hand, was harder. I knew Daisy, for one thing, and for another she was going to die. Then again, she was spiritual. She practiced a discipline based on acceptance and letting go. Think of all those Zen tales in which monks get hit on the head or step in shit and respond by finding enlightenment and laughing.

Still. She was going to *die*.

The card I chose had a picture of berries on the front. Not flowers, which might bring to mind a funeral bouquet. I stared down at the inside of the card for a long while before writing that I thought of her often, that my thoughts were with her now. I wrote that I thought she was special.

What the fuck can you say?

Because the mind will believe anything, I told myself a card meant more than spoken words. Because recipients can *keep* the cards. A written message is forever, can be held between the hands, unlike speech. Spoken words like rainbows vanish into thin air unless you save them artificially with a machine. So say you visit—when you leave, the words you said might just as well never have been. A card, by contrast: the recipient can stand it upright anywhere, gazing at it across the room for reassurance or clasping it in the middle of the night. Plus, cards offer two choices: you can look at the nice picture on the front or at the soothing message within.

Cop-out.

Hallmark makes cards for most occasions. But which occasion is this, what do you call it when you are sending a card to say, *So you're going to die!* Or, *You're going to die and I am sending this card because I am afraid to visit you.*

She wrote back thanking me for my kind thoughts. With her exquisite signature, with a daisy over the *i* in Daisy. She was like that.

I RAN INTO her a few weeks later in the Y. She looked a little swollen but not sick. Wearing nylon shorts and a stretchy tank top, she had one shoe up on the bench and was tying its laces. I asked her how she was.

She said *better,* in a tone that meant *better but still going to die,* but with a shrug. It was so Zen. She said, *The trouble started in my tummy.* Daisy used words like that—tootsies, noggin, tummy. *Then I had some tests. And wasn't I surprised!* She stretched her leg behind her, as most ladies her age cannot do.

Well, I was shocked to hear, I said.

Yeah, Daisy said, stretching her other leg. *Me, too.*

She asked how I was. *Say hi to that blue-eyed man of yours.*

I THOUGHT OF it afterward as The Last Time I Saw Daisy Alive. I thought: She made it easy for me. She was calm and cool. She is a lady and she sits *zazen,* and I could go and see her but it is no longer necessary because that time at the Y was good-bye and Daisy made it OK.

Three or four months after I saw her in the Y I was on the checkout line at the supermarket. I was nearly up to the cashier, flipping through tabloids, when I looked up and saw Daisy.

She looked terrible. Her hair was thin and greasy and the

bloat was worse. Her skin was the stippled white of chickens in butcher shops. She was not smiling, looking instead the way people sick in public do, as if to say, *Just go to hell*. Her purchase was completed. From one hand swung a string bag with what looked liked a box of corn flakes and some apples in it. She was walking toward the door in a trajectory that took her right past me. If she looked sideways she would see me there. If I waved or said hi.

I said nothing and faced the magazine rack. I am pretty sure she never saw me. She walked within five feet of me but I really think she never saw me. Did she, though? Maybe she did.

MY MOTHER DOES not have this problem. She does not avoid the dying. She phones them. She walks right up to them. She goes out shopping for them and brings them boxes of what they ask for or what she knows would be nice for them. Sweaters and soup and fruit. Earrings that look nice with their wigs. Amusingly shaped crackers. Not just once but *all the time*, and when the patient feels too sick to talk or too ugly to be seen my mother drives up to the house, sets the items on the porch, rings the bell and politely drives away. My friend Carleen, who loathed her father, remembers how happy he was when my mother arrived those last weeks of his life with cans of chicken-and-stars soup, which he loved.

My mother says this is no special talent, but it is. She says she is just as afraid of death as anyone. But how can that be, when she is always the first to call when a friend has just received a terrible diagnosis? *What do you need?* she asks, and she means it. She can stay on the phone for hours even in the middle of the night, or she can show up in a flash. If they want to cry or describe certain procedures, she will never flinch. If they want distraction, she thinks of news to tell. If they want to be silent but still not alone, she sits mute on their sofas or at home holding her telephone.

Nor does she call or visit any of them only once, as some might do, imagining our duty done. She pops back in, right till the end. How does she do it? She is not so nice to everyone on principle. She can be shockingly curt with shop clerks and strangers on the phone. She says, maybe being kind to the dying is a selfish way of bargaining with God to spare *her* life. But I am just as eager as the next girl to make such deals, and yet—this is a line I tell myself time after time to cross, and then I turn and run time after time.

IN MY DESK drawer, inches from my hand this very minute, is a parcel of shiny gold wrapping paper folded into a parcel two inches square, Scotch taped. Inside are ashes. Handed to me by a young man who was folding hundreds like it at a white-draped table—ash swirled in the air, smearing his suit—the parcel contains what was once part of the body of Brian Williams.

Brian Williams was a talented artist who specialized in baroque landscapes dotted with temples, nudes, and poplars. His paintings hung in office buildings all over San Francisco, and every year he led art-museum tours to Italy. He designed tarot cards. I interviewed him once for a magazine article, and for the next fifteen years after that he always waved when he sped past me on his bicycle, flashing a brilliant smile. I saw him at the wedding of mutual friends—we sat together, eating cake, and he said with a sly wink that one of his eyes was made of glass. AIDS had given him five varieties of cancer, the latest of which was ocular. *But here I am!* he beamed, looking divine. We were on laughing terms but not exactly intimate, which is why it surprised me one year later to be included among the guests Brian had specified must be invited to his funeral.

In the church, children performed baroque music and his boyfriend stood beside a massive urn that Brian had designed himself and said, *I loved a genius.* After the service, each guest was given a small package of the ashes to scatter where we thought best. The idea was for him to be everywhere beautiful. Putting the parcel in my purse—feeling weird, handling it—I vowed to take it to the beach.

But it is in my drawer. *Part of Brian, or different parts mixed up, is in my drawer.* I have been to the beach five or six times since receiving the parcel but I forgot to bring it every time. It lies there with the pens and spiral pads, business cards acquired and ignored. I forget for long periods that it is there, and now its shine is all rubbed off along the folds. One of these days it will have to go somewhere, but see what a rat I am? Dodging the dying *and*—that poor sweet man—the dead. See what a rat I am?

2.

regret

REMEMBER WHAT YOU thought you ought to do—what perhaps you vowed to do and perhaps told others you were going to do, then put off? I'll get around to it, you said and then you put it off again. You kept saying next time, next time. You meant to get around to it. You really did, you told yourself you would, you promised, and then it was too late.

Regret burns like corrosive quicksand.

And nothing begets regret like death.

The kind of regret that death begets entails another person, someone to whom you wanted to say something or for whom you wanted to do something, someone to whom you owed a favor or an explanation or a confession or who owed such a thing to you. Someone between whom and yourself lay unfinished business, a covenant, a pact, a possibility. A mystery, a troth, a crime that will never be solved, a truce you never can draw because he or she is dead. And it is now that you discover what forever means, and that *never say never* is a pretty theory but silly. Never exists, and it makes you pay.

Regret begins while that other party to whom something is owed or who owes you something is still alive. Regret starts in the aftermaths of fights, the torpor of unspoken passions, in the leas of secrets and misunderstandings, the marshes of unasked questions. While that other party lives, you can keep saying *someday* and put off the rapprochement, the request, conquest, confession, or duel, *simply because you can.* As long as that clock ticks and you both breathe.

But then.

Then death pulls out the stops, yanks off the gloves. Death shatters fantasy and hope. And all you wished to say and do, and all you wished to fix or solve for good or ill, mercies you sought, revenge, all that you wished to prove, are snatched away with that last breath. And now you cannot say a word. Not. One. Minuscule. Word.

Too late.

You can say *never* all day long.

Death renders all points moot, the points that geometrically plot your regret. Yet the more moot they are, the darker and more permanent. And all your would-haves vaporize. All the king's horses, and all the king's men—

Too late, you say.

Too late.

A MAN NAMED Robert once lived in Paris.

I know that much but almost nothing more. Living in Paris, speaking French, he said not *RAH-burt* as we do in English but *Roe-BAIR*. After the war he called himself Bob, because after the war he would live in America. This is where I knew him, as a skinny old man who spoke little and with an accent and, when eating Chinese food, plucked bits of meat out of his mouth between his fingers and laid the bits with disgust at the edge of his plate.

Before the war, he called himself Roe-BAIR—but how did he pronounce his name in private, addressing himself and no one French? He was not French, though he pretended to be French. In his head, when Robert chided himself, consoled himself or warned himself of anything, what did he call himself? His name was really Robert, but how would the Czechs pronounce it? In his hometown, whose name and location I also do not know. A shtetl? Prague? I do not know, and there is someone I could ask but she is ninety-one and at the moment has two broken arms.

Or is this another excuse from my big bag of excuses?

Surely a Czech *r* does not sound so uvular as the French *r*, that half-swallowed-caramel *ggh*.

Nor do I know when he arrived in France or why. Czechoslovakia was perhaps seeming less and less hospitable to Jews. He was fleeing an annulled marriage, I know that: arranged by his family and hers, yet within days of the wedding she proved to be insane. How did he find out, I would like to know. Was it in bed? I only know of this wife because my aunt Ruby, who was his wife later, showed me a stack of embroidered linens in her house in Florida. White on white but yellowed with age, they were from that first dowry—said Ruby in passing, searching in the bureau for a pair of beach towels.

Were the linens monogrammed? If so, was it his initials or hers, or both of theirs, entwined? I do not know and will not know.

Perhaps fleeing the shame of that bad match, he went to Paris and opened a butcher shop. Was it the family trade, passed from father to son? He exchanged his Czech surname for a generic one, Stein. He ran the shop with a partner. Robert married again.

Whether his second wife was a Frenchwoman or, like him, a foreigner, I do not know. Was she Jewish or Catholic? They had a baby girl. The names of wife and child I do not know. I could find out, but there again that would mean asking.

War broke out. This part of the story, the big picture, you can learn anywhere, in movies and encyclopedias. *The war in France.* What I wonder but never will know is how and when Robert made his plan: to save himself. This is the part that makes me think his wife was Christian, as his plan left her exposed, with the baby, in Paris. She must have felt safe.

Robert joined the French army, pretending to be a Gentile. None of his comrades could know—with his bunkmates and messmates, Robert must have faked a Catholic past, but how? Reciting bits of Latin heard through church doors?

He passed. Perhaps he explained his accent by saying he was born in Switzerland. His unit fought a while, then was captured. When the Nazis learned that he was a butcher, he became a special prisoner with kitchen privileges. He stashed scraps in his shirt and sneaked them to his mates.

How long was he a POW, and where? I do not know. When the war ended, how long did it take him to get home? I do not know, but when he got there his partner was gone. His butcher shop was closed. His wife and child had vanished and Robert never saw them again.

• • •

I do not know. Ask me nothing because I do not know. I tell myself that I could fly to Florida. My aunt Ruby with her two broken arms might tell me more. But it would come from her, not him, and that is *not the same*. I tell myself it is something at least. I tell myself to go.

I tell myself a lot of things.

He moved to Manhattan, called himself Bob, and opened a new butcher shop. He met my aunt, who was a widow, at a Jewish club. This meant little to me at age eight, when my father at our dinner table said, *My sister hooked a Frenchman*. What was it to me? I did not know my aunt. She lived three thousand miles away and she was even older than my dad.

They came and spent a week with us. I do not think I spoke a word to Bob. He was so quiet, in his pale green polyester golf pants, and he did that awful thing with Chinese food.

Bob is particular about his meat, my aunt said with a cheery smile.

I could have talked to him, but at eight how was I to know how much there was to know? I knew about a war. I knew about the Holocaust. But the details were fuzzy and so far away. Bob did not speak to me. I wonder now, was it because little girls brought to mind his own—and the fact that, though he had tried to find her through all sorts of agencies, she was lost to him for good? Were my hair ribbons more than he could bear?

Ruby made overtures. She hugged me, bit my cheek, left teeth-marks, squealed, *I want to eat you up!*

Ten years later, I stayed with them in Florida. I was traveling with my roommate to the Caribbean and their house was on the way. Ruby and Bob took us to a museum, where in a room full of Impressionist paintings I said something about Bob being French.

I'm not French, he said. *I'm from Czechoslovakia.*

You could have knocked me over.

What, you speak three *languages?* I said.

Four, Bob said, *if you count Yiddish.*

AND THEN AND there it could have started, me extracting the story of Bob. Extracting it, recording it, writing it down—a story of the war, a Jew, a man, survival, loss. A story for the ages, a tale of passion and blood and tears.

What a book it could have been. Should have been.

I could also have come to know my uncle. We might have hit it off. He might have liked to know that a young person cared about his past. The painful story would be hard to tell, but I would coax him, tell him that millions would be touched and illuminated. Millions would clamor to read his tale of madness and flight, crisis and strategy, deceit and redemption. *I* would. Wouldn't you?

He might have turned me down flat, said the past was the past and better left behind. People his age were always saying that—no surprise after what they went through. Look ahead, to Cadillacs and grilled-cheese sandwiches on Wonder bread. He might have demurred and that would have been OK, a shame but OK. But he never got the chance, because I never asked.

It would have been so easy. I was there, all week. A spiral pad and pen were in my bag. Each night after dinner—the four of us women around a card table, watching TV—he sat on the sofa in striped Bermuda shorts, reading golf magazines. The nights loomed long, mocking our polite smiles as we sought ways to fill the humid hours, as moths self-immolated on the porch light. He sat, sipping iced Sanka. He was right there.

It was that week when Ruby, seeking towels for a trip to the beach, showed me the linens from Czechoslovakia. *Whatever happened to that crazy woman? Hitler probably got her,* Ruby said. *Did you know, we went to Paris three years ago so Bob could look in the old city records for his daughter and his second wife. Were they killed or did his wife run away with someone else? We spent ten days. You know what he found? Poor Bob. Nothing,* bupkes, *zilch.*

WHY DID I simply take the towels, thank her, and go? What do eighteen-year-olds think about? Did I not realize that the tale had everything? You could not beat occupied France for a setting, prisoners of war for characters.

I could have caught it in my spiral pad, filling page after page till it was full. Going to Eckerd's down the street, buying another pad.

We could have sat there side by side, his brown legs ribbed with fat veins, my legs pale. Ruby would have brought Fiddle Faddle on a tray, I know she would have. I would have asked her to ask him the most awkward question of all: how, in the army and the camp, did he hide being circumcised? That was the only thing I could not ask. The rest I would. We would have stayed up late yakking like best friends, he and I.

It never crossed my mind.

Not all that week in Florida. Not after flying home.

Sure, it seems so obvious now. So meant to be.

It never crossed my mind until thirteen years later.

This is it, I thought. This is the greatest idea in the world.

A lot of books were coming out by then about the war, the Holocaust, miraculous escapes. Sounds like a plan, I told myself. This is the time.

BUT IT WAS not, because I put it off. I kept telling myself to call, to visit them in Florida. Ruby loved company. I kept putting it off.

It was a plan held in reserve, a secret plan, ready at any moment to spring into action.

It was so simple, so solid that I found it very easy to put off. To say it was what I would do next summer. Or next winter. One phone call and *ready, set, go.*

Count the years like chickens on a fence, no call.

His first stroke made him an amnesiac. He did not know who Ruby was. He spoke only in Czech.

And all the linens, all the strudels, all the Citroëns and sirloin and nine-irons mingled in his head. Those names and faces once remembered, names recorded *somewhere*, surely, faces photographed—a mercy of sorts as they spun into a blur. All the lips he once loved, speaking four languages if you count Yiddish, and of course you do, and the rest of his thoughts—an omelet now, a pulp.

His second stroke turned his Czech into a child's Czech. His third stroke silenced him. His fourth killed him outright.

IF I HAD asked him and he had refused, there would be nothing to regret.

But he said neither yes nor no and never will. It is the not-asking that stings, that sears, that blisters. Regret is a sickness caused by what you did not do and say and where you did not go. In this regard, it is a kind of backwards sickness, spawned by nothingness, inaction, silence. Yet it burns as badly as the kind of condition that comes from something you *did*.

The causes of regret are sometimes sweet and sometimes sour, sometimes noble, sometimes mercenary.

What we regret:

I know a woman whose mother went into the hospital after suffering chest pains. The doctors decided to keep her there and monitor her heart. It was fifty years ago, so neither diagnostic nor surgical techniques were very far advanced. The daughter promised her mother that she would visit every day and for the first three days she did. On the fourth day she was going to go but her boyfriend called from the university. One of his classes had been canceled and he had an hour free. Could he come over?

She looked at the clock. But of course he could. He was brilliant, he was talented, he was Gerald, and he was just two blocks away.

And she could go to the hospital afterward. She could slip in right before visiting hours ended. She could get there before the patients had their dinners.

She and Gerald had sex—not the first time, not the last. Not the best time, not the worst—not that any of those times were all that great. But it was the time she would always remember, the one she would never forget, because that day, that very *hour*, her mother died.

I know a man who began an online courtship while his mother was dying. It was an exciting courtship and promising—he felt that someday he would meet this woman who lived thousands of miles away but whom he had never seen in person, and that when they met it would be magic. But he never breathed a word about her to his mother. This was typical of him. He had always been shy and secretive about relationships. Part of him wanted to share his excitement with his mother, but he could not break his own resolve. He watched her die. A year later he met his online girlfriend in the flesh. It *was* magic. Now they are married, with a baby. His mother could have met her future daughter-in-law, the future mother of her grandson—could at least have seen the young stranger's picture on a screen. It would have been so easy. A word, a flick of the wrist, a click. But no.

I know a man whose wife wanted to travel, though he always nixed her plans—because he was busy at work, because he did not want to miss the Superbowl, because he did not like to fly. She was always bringing home handfuls of colorful brochures from travel agencies, glossy with their pictures of beaches and cathedrals, of forests and archeological sites, with middle-aged couples just like themselves striding laden with shopping bags along cobblestone streets, and waving from the decks of cruise ships. She made it all seem so easy, writing sample itineraries on sheets of graph paper, and always including activities she knew would appeal to him: *Tuesday—Visit Happy Valley racetrack! Sunday—Biergarten!* He knew how special this was—his buddies were always describing vacations that had been spent doing only what their wives wanted, or their wives and kids, *without a thought for the guy footing the bill,* while *his* wife was more than willing to tour a stock exchange or sit all evening in a sports bar. She was. And one day he would show her how grateful he could be and how obliging, one day he would surprise her and say, *Yes, sure, honey, wherever you'd like to go, just say the word. No time like the present.* He would hug her and say it someday, one of these days, on exactly the right day, maybe their anniversary or maybe her birthday. But he never said it, not once, and one night as she drove home with a purse full of brochures, her car skidded on ice and wrapped around a tree and she died.

I know a couple whose daughter killed herself at eighteen. The overdose she took after fighting with a boyfriend might have been accidental—a threat, a ploy for attention. Her parents asked themselves, and are still asking themselves thirty years later, whether her death was a result of their permissiveness. They had always supported her desire to experiment. In those days it was still unusual for girls to start sleeping with boys at thirteen, but she did. Her mother took her to the doctor for birth-control pills. It was unusual then as now for teenage girls to date grown-up men. Discovering the affair, her father wanted to charge her lover with statutory rape—the lover who taunted her, the lover who mocked her, the lover who torched her self-esteem. The girl's father wanted to charge that man with statutory rape and run him out of her life, but he never did.

When my friend Catrina was starting her new career as a Hollywood talent agent, she wrote to her grandmother every week. The old lady lived in a tiny country town, without a phone. *I kept making up excuses not to go up there,* Catrina says now. *I kept telling myself I was being a good granddaughter by writing letters.* In a family dominated by stern ex-soldiers and miners, Catrina's grandmother was the only fun-loving one. *She was the nonjudgmental adult who would say, Hey, let's run down the street with no shoes on!* She was also the only member of the family to whom Catrina wanted to introduce her fiancé. She and Patrick kept making tentative plans to fly out to the country, but Catrina scuppered them at the last minute every time. *One Friday I wrote Gram a letter asking if we could come and stay for a week,* she says. The next day Catrina's grandmother was discovered dead of a hemorrhage in her spotless kitchen.

It is ten years later and Catrina volunteers at a retirement home, where she leads a drama troupe. *I know it's because I'm trying to make up for not giving time to my grandmother—and for my grandfather, who died a few years before she did. I'm an old-person magnet. They always like me and I like them. They talk to me.* Often she brings little gifts, prettily wrapped, for favorite residents at the home. *I know it's payback,* Catrina says.

MY FRIEND SHERRY was the last member of her family to talk with her father. He was in the hospital after a major heart attack and lay holding her hand. His fingers in hers were as cool and slack as custard. She was telling him that if anything should happen to him, she would take care of her mother.

He opened his eyes and gazed at her. His throat was damaged and it cost him great effort to speak.

I'm scared, he said.

She squeezed his hand. There were a million things she could have said. She had studied psychology in college.

It's OK, she said. Later she thought she should have said, *You're scared? Of course you are, Dad, it must be so scary to die but we'll be here with you.* Later she thought she should have said, *Tell me how you feel, Dad.* Later she lambasted herself for not addressing his terror head-on, for not comforting him. It was his moment, after all, *his* deathbed, and she was the only one he had to tell. His eyes twitched when he said it.

It's OK, she'd said: generic, pertaining to no one in particular, deliberately vague as to the referent for *it*. It's OK? What is? Nothing is, not for you, not right now.

She said those two words only. In the silence afterward, he whispered, *Well, sweetie, I guess you better go.* She did. She left him there shortly before he went into a coma.

Now she says she could not handle his being afraid. She *never* could handle her father's fear, not when she was small and not at the end. The thing about deathbeds, Sherry says, is that they don't change our personalities. He was her *father*, his job was to comfort *her*. She had spent her whole life shielding herself from seeing him as vulnerable. She had never seen him cry or scream or shake with fear. And she could not start then. He had never sought consolation before and she had never given it. Those two words mock her now. They haunt her: *it's OK it's OK it's OK,* like the futile blasts of party horns.

The worst regret of all is when the death was actually, or arguably, your fault. Directly, indirectly. If you had been more observant. If you had arrived home on time. If you had not been drunk. This is when regret, the dread of what you did not do, turns into guilt, the dread of what you did. Which is another story altogether.

DEATH TRANSFORMS REGRET in an instant from a sickness that you can cure into one you cannot. Suddenly you know the meaning of never and forever, because you are stuck with them both. In retrospect you keep thinking up more and more things you should have done. How different it all would have been if you had only said that word or made that call or paid that visit, or acquired comic-book superpowers at the crucial moment: X-ray vision, for instance, or the strength to lift twenty thousand pounds, or fly, or run a million miles an hour. A magic pill. Clairvoyance. Time travel, back to the days of "Cherry Pink and Apple Blossom White," back to the days of "The Purple People Eater" or "Jungle Fever" or "Walk Like an Egyptian."

It would be very Zen to just let go. The very moment you realize that he or she around whom your regret circles is dead and can no longer give or forgive, just stop. Right there and then. Your would-have-could-have-should-haves are as ineffectual as currency from a nation that no longer exists: Rhodesia, for instance, or Yugoslavia. Tell yourself what is done is done—or undone, as it were. Or weren't.

Because at that point all the wishes in the world are suddenly revealed for what they are: hot air.

So for your own good the best thing would be to recognize the error of your ways, the folly of saying *someday*, and take this as a lesson. Make a vow. Next time it will be different. Yes, there *will* be a next time. And no, next times are not a boundless quantity. They do run out.

But most of us cannot face facts. Regret is about blame and guilt. To fob off some of your own guilt, you blame the other party:

He never listened to me anyway.

She was always in such a bad mood that I never got a chance.

He never had the time.

I was finally going to say 'I love you' the last time I saw her but she was watching Montel *and wouldn't turn it off.*

He started it.

This pales after a while because it is, in a very nearly literal sense, flogging a dead horse. Your conscience says in its nagging voice that the responsibility for your own inactions is yours alone. Then regret turns completely insular. Regret waggles in your face some harsh inescapable realities about yourself. I failed to connect with my uncle and hear his interesting story because (in no particular order) I am a *space cadet*;

I am *slow on the uptake*; I am *lazy*; I *procrastinate*. When regret strikes, you are a dog chasing its tail, a capsule orbiting in space. Death makes you see the power you had all along, the power to move mountains, join together, tear asunder, admit, expunge, love, divulge, divest. In your hands this power vibrated, in your mouth. Now it is gone and who are you, a big impotent windbag.

This is what we say, and talk and talk and talk as we might now, we cannot inject words into the past. We cannot put what we should have said into a time machine so that forever, now, those words will have been said. Talk as we might now, talk talk talk, it cannot penetrate the mire between now and then, between life and death.

The things we should have said:

My friend Sara watched her mother grow sicker and sicker with inoperable cancer. Eventually her mother would be unable to get out of bed, would go into the hospital one last time and wind up on life support, which her children would decide to turn off. But before that—*after* she'd been sick for years, but shortly before that—Sara and her mother went shopping for swimsuits one day. They chatted happily like pals. There was a moment in the fitting room when it was just the two of them, alone and intimate, and Sara could have said, *OK, are you ready to die?* It would have been the right thing at the right time. Someone had to ask her, says Sara, whose sister was in such denial as to never mention illness, hospitals, or death. She could not ask, though. It would not come out. *I'm still amazed*, she says. *I'm such an articulate person, a pontificator, but I couldn't say a word about how she might be feeling or what it meant.* They went about their day together, then they went about the next. It was not long before they were all in the hospital and her mother lay blinking in bed unable to speak. No one could discern whether she was too far gone to understand. Sara said nothing then, either, and then they pulled the plug. *Talk about a sin of omission*, Sara says.

When my friend Jamie was a boy, his father was a tyrant whose rages made the family afraid of him. *It turned us all inward,* Jamie recalls. A tense dynamic established itself, mind games by which his father would say, *I love you, son,* and it was obvious that Jamie was supposed to say, *I love you, too,* but he would not. It became second nature just to absorb those three words and not reply. Jamie would wonder sometimes, *What am I trying to do? Punish the guy?* He was. *I didn't want my dad to have the satisfaction.* As he grew older, Jamie found ways to say it without really saying it: sneaking it onto Christmas cards or at the ends of letters: *Love, Jamie.* He was nearly thirty when his father was diagnosed with myeloma. That was bad enough but cruelly ironic, because the two of them were for the first time in their lives starting to develop a real rapport. His father had moved to the countryside and Jamie would visit him there. Sitting on the deck under the stars, they had just begun to open up. Now, hearing from his stepmother how sick his father was and how swiftly he was degenerating, Jamie rushed cross-country to the hospital. There his father lay, withered and pale.

I kissed him on the forehead. I hadn't kissed him in a long time. His father looked up and said, *I love you.*

Jamie said nothing.

All his life he had held those words back, could never say them then—or now. As Sherry says, deathbeds do not transform the living into saints and sages—into anything at all besides themselves. Standing there silently, the clock ticking away, Jamie scolded himself: *You bastard, Jamie, you will hate yourself for this forever.*

And, a little bit, he does.

3.

greed

WHEN MY FRIEND Heather and I were both nineteen, her mother started having mysterious health problems. The doctors scheduled her for a hysterectomy, but warned the family that they might find something even worse inside her than what the X-rays showed. Before going to the hospital, Heather's mother walked around the house with a packet of little white stickers. To each of her most prized possessions—the candlesticks, the vases, the porcelain, the Hummel figurines—she affixed a sticker inscribed with one of the names of her four children. Her collection was no grander than what you might find in any average middle-class ranch-style home, but she wanted to make sure that, in the event of her death, each item would go to whichever child she believed in her heart would love it best. The task took several hours, but when it was done she felt satisfied, put away her pen, and went to church.

After checking her mother into the hospital a few days later, Heather drove back to the empty house. Letting herself in, she walked from room to room through the eerie silence switching the stickers around. *What? Mom gave Donald the Royal Copenhagen plates? I'll fix that. And as for this Venetian glass clown . . .*

The stickers came off easily. Heather allotted herself the best and most precious things, then she slipped quietly out of the house. On her way back to the hospital she stopped by to see me. She was flushed and laughing.

I won!

Her giggles came out shivery and thin, like tinsel, which I knew meant that they were subterfuge. Heather was accustomed to besting her brothers and sister. Cribbage and football and Risk—she always won whatever games they played. She took winning for granted.

Guess what? Now I'm gonna get the Wedgwood!

But her smile held a glint of horror. Heather rubbed her hands together and shifted her weight. *I felt like a burglar in there.* She was scaring herself. Watching herself change right before her own eyes from someone who mocked material possessions—she always sneered at my stuffed closet—into a claim-jumper, a cheat, a thief. Who was this stranger? What lycanthropy was this? *I got the silver peppermill!* I watched her watch herself.

You are minding your own business, right in the middle of your life, when someone dies. And then you are minding your own business, right in the middle of grief, when out of nowhere comes a prickling in your scalp, a tingling in your palms, a jerking knee. At first their meaning puzzles you. Impatience?

Dread? It feels a bit like both, a bit like hunger, too. And then you realize: it is desire.

You ask yourself how death can make you crave. But there it is, that lurch.

You want.

And out of nowhere, as if displayed on a wide conveyor belt, under a floodlight, *things* invade your grief.

As the condolences drone on and on, desire sizzles and frets. The thing about desire, that spinal *getgetget*, is that it is alive. A contrast that, given the circumstances, can astound. Loss peels you raw. Your resistance is low.

So in a blink you are battling your fellow survivors for glass clowns and bank accounts, for property deeds and original-issue vintage Barbie dolls. And *they* battle *you*, scheming in their mourning clothes. The same family who—back then, long ago—watched *Antiques Roadshow* together, musing lightly about the contents of Aunt Ellen's attic, now race to find the keys and reach it first.

As those condolences drone on and on, you wonder where in your apartment the taxidermied swordfish ought to go. You are mentally wearing pearls. You fight the yearning and the impulses, you call them crass and inappropriate, but they persist. You tell yourself, This is ridiculous. You tell yourself, Stop this. Then, throwing down your gloves, you rush into the fray, telling yourself, *I'm worth it, man. It's mine.*

· · ·

GOLD WILL NOT turn to dust as bones do. Linen will not bloat and burst like skin. Porcelain, unlike organs, remains sleek and firm. A set of cutlery will never die.

As AN ONLY child, I have managed to stay out of all such tournaments. I have never had to fight over an inheritance, and I never will, which is good, because I always lose fights. One set of my grandparents was already dead before I was born. The other set had nothing when they died that I desired back then—though now I wish I had the china cookie jar shaped like a whale with Jonah perched on top; his little body in its dungarees and red-and-white-striped shirt and peaked cap was the handle with which you removed the lid. I hold no claims on anything belonging to my aunts, who have children and grandchildren and great-grandchildren of their own. In all these years no one has ever claimed me as a protégée and promised me a treasure —*All these geodes will be yours!* No one has taken me under his or her wing. Nothing has been bequeathed to me. I am the favorite of no one.

It is no crime to want a legacy. It is nothing more or less than pragmatic. Belongings have lost their owner: someone might as well collect them, just as you would pick up money or a bracelet you found in the street. In our world, those who die forfeit their wealth. This is not ancient Egypt, where the dead were entombed with all their possessions, to wear their clothes and drive oxen and row boats and plant and reap wheat in the rich plains of the afterworld.

But—are the objects of desire worth resorting to trickery? Worth lowering oneself to acts that give your rivals little choice but to plunge into a lifetime of suspicion, resentment, mistrust? How much are the spoils worth? Are they worth more, or less, than your personal relationships henceforth?

The things we say:

He got it all.

He took it all.

That ring he gave his fiancée—you recognized it, right?

Of course I did. That whore.

BEING ANYWHERE NEAR a death puts you into a state of shock. And shock is not merely a word but an actual medical condition, a response to trauma. In shock, your blood pressure plummets. Your pulse races. Your thoughts judder and skip. One symptom of shock, which rescue workers notice right away, is a fixation on the trivial—because the brain is overwhelmed by what is *really* going on. Against catastrophe, the brain shuts down. It feels no pain. This is both bad and good. After falling and breaking a leg in the kitchen, the injured person crawls around on the floor for hours in a daze, not calling 911 because he doesn't want the paramedics to see his unflushed toilet, or the dirty dishes in the sink.

Shock is the great distractor, the hand puppet waggling in the corner chortling, *Look over HERE!* The night my head went through a windshield—blood was gushing down my face—I spent the ambulance ride telling knock-knock jokes. *Orange. Orange who? Orange you glad I didn't say banana?* I asked the rescue crew whether the color of blood suited my hair. I kept thinking, My shirt, my shirt, it's stained, where can I buy another shirt?

Victims dragged out of burning houses will run back inside to rescue their Tom Jones CDs.

In shock, you think of things.

IN SHOCK, YOU cling.

When my friend Erin's bachelor uncle died, she went with her mother and sisters—his only surviving relatives—to the condo where he had lived in semi-seclusion. In the bedroom of this secretive middle-aged man, the women were surprised to find feminine clothes and accessories. Most of these expensive gowns and wigs and purses and shoes and hair ornaments were in immaculate condition, and clearly had never been worn outdoors.

Erin and her mother and sisters methodically assembled their findings on the couch and the bed.

Dibs on the Prada bags, said Sandy.

Dibs on all these perfumes, Erin said.

Dibs on the leather coat, said Caroline.

Sandy protested. *You live in Hawaii! You don't need a leather coat!*

Girrrls, said their mother, making a pile of Hermès scarves for herself.

It was then that they found the pearls.

In a black satin box, in a bureau drawer: a long strand of perfect white pearls.

Caroline slid the leather coat over to Sandy's side of the bed.

Make you a deal, she said. *You guys take everything else. I just want the pearls.*

It seemed fair. The pearls were clearly the single most valuable item in the room, but there was so much else to divide among the other three. Caroline sealed the deal by reminding them that she was the only divorced one among them, thus had suffered the most, thus deserved the most beautiful thing.

They all went home with their treasures the next day.

About a year later Erin's mother was diagnosed with lymphoma. The doctors said she had anywhere between six months and five years.

She called Caroline and asked her for the pearls.

I need something, sweetheart, to make me feel good.

Caroline said nothing, then cleared her throat.

We had a deal, said Caroline. *You said.*

But sweetheart, said her mother.

No, said Caroline.

IT IS A strange transaction, the transfer of assets to the living from the dead. It is a business at once tender and crude, a kind of grave-robbing, a kind of grace. The presence of lawyers, executors, and wills makes it easier. But wills can be harsh. William Shakespeare left virtually nothing to his wife, Anne, and younger daughter Judith, while his elder daughter Susanna and her family inherited his money, two houses, and "all my barns, stables, orchards, gardens, lands"—it was his choice and he left his survivors to contemplate what it might mean.

OBJECTS ARE COMPENSATION. Paltry, sad—a Hummel goose-girl in exchange for Mom. But several thousand years of civilization have drummed into our heads this need for compensation. In a complicated world where life is evanescent, where people disappear, and where gods are fickle, we have come to depend on an honest wage. Work and get paid. And watching someone die, having to summon the courage to go on living without a certain person, is the hardest work in the world.

Polite society would say you cannot compare *this* kind of work—the work of worry, sorrow, horror, and seeing the worst—to other kinds, say stockbrokering or highway repair. Polite society would say you get no compensation for *this* kind of work: that a caregiver or mourner is just a volunteer, performing out of love, out of a sense of sacrifice. Polite society would say that life is hard, so just buck up.

The trauma (and thus the accumulated billable hours) of dying spreads outward from the dying person to the primary caregiver, then in a widening set of concentric circles to the caregiver's loved ones and their loved ones. Those in every circle suffer, each to a different degree, and suffering, as the modern world has come to interpret it, merits remuneration. It is not as simple a matter as punching a timecard and waiting for the check. But is it all that different, really? Being near a death leaves you burnt out, depleted, stressed. Being near a death means having to control yourself, having to battle your impulses to scream or flee, having to interact with others under dire conditions. If that is not labor, then what is? The mind is wired to calculate. If there are spoils, divide them, wrap them up, and take them home.

· · ·

[GREED]

EVEN SO, THIS is no party. Collecting wages from the dead feels inherently creepy, like raiding a tomb or yanking watches off the wrists of fallen soldiers. Inherited things carry the sad taint of forsaken souvenirs. Remnants in steel and silk and porcelain and gem and cash and realty of a life, a story over. The song asks: *Is that all there is?* Yes. It is.

Mommy and Daddy went to heaven and all I got was this lousy timeshare in Boca Raton.

After the funeral you look around a room and see the figurines and the piano, and coffee mugs that say MAUREEN and KISS ME and THE FASTER I GO, THE BEHINDER I GET. Packing items into boxes, clearing out closets and bank accounts and safe-deposit boxes turns you into Ali Baba, into Jason or one of his Argonauts hunting for hidden treasure, and into yourself, scrambling for whatever will shine and weigh heavily in your hands and fill that emptiness.

MY EX-BOYFRIEND VAL grew up in the desert. When I knew him, most of his family still lived in a series of houses spread out across several acres on the outskirts of a town near a military base. He brought me to visit them twice. The first time, we stayed with his grandmother, Elva, in her pink bungalow. She was ninety-four. We all ate chicken pies. The next time was six years later, when the family gathered for Elva's hundredth birthday party. Val's parents were there, and his little brother, and his aunt Bonnie and her two teenage daughters, and his bachelor uncle Jess who was an electrician at the nearby army base. We all exchanged hellos and the self-conscious nods of partygoers who would never otherwise be together in the same room. The cake had a hundred tiny candles. Val's uncle was wearing a kilt. Elva shook all of our hands and thanked us for coming, but would someone mind telling her why we were here? And would someone please help her into the bedroom, because the TV was in there and she wanted to watch Dinah Shore.

That was all. I never saw her again. Elva died within the year, and when it happened Val's parents told him not to bother coming all the way to the desert for the funeral, it was just the family anyway and a quick cremation.

Three days later they called him again. That time, they had something to ask.

The night Elva died, Bonnie let herself into the pink bungalow with a list of items to collect—items that she had coveted for years, some of which she would distribute to the rest of the family but only after saving the top seven or eight things for herself. It was her just reward, she reasoned, for having helped Elva more than the others did, always picking up her prescriptions at the drugstore and making sure she had ready-made Seal-a-Meal dinners in her freezer. And after all, it was Bonnie who'd discovered Elva dead in the shower.

Along with the gold pen-and-pencil set and wide-screen TV, on her list was a diamond ring. Elva had worn it when she was a young bride, but it became too ostentatious a thing for an aging lady to wear in a small desert town. A few years before her death, Elva had shown Bonnie where the ring was: in a varnished cherrywood chest with the rest of her jewelry. Now, picking through the chest, Bonnie found the rhinestone pins and fake pearls but not the ring. She took everything out of the box and put it back in again and then began rifling, increasingly panicked, through Elva's desk and dresser drawers. Finding no ring, she searched in the odd sorts of places where old ladies might cache things: eyeglass cases, jiggers, and the freezer. But as the search came up fruitless, a picture emerged in Bonnie's mind of where the ring must be, of who must have taken it.

Me.

She assembled a family meeting to make sure that none of the others had the ring, which of course they did not. She told them her theory. It seemed so plausible. Who was I—the girlfriend of the favorite grandchild. The only question was, what ruse had I used? During that birthday party, had I whispered to the demented Elva that I was poor? Or had I merely found it in its cherrywood chest and swiped it?

This was the question Val's mother and father asked him.

Hang on a sec, Val said and lifted my hand.

I did not have the ring. I never saw the ring. I never even knew there was a ring.

I never saw his family again.

Eight months after Elva died, the pink bungalow was for sale. Bonnie was clearing out Elva's bedroom closet to donate its contents to Goodwill. As she folded an old party dress, Bonnie felt something hard and circular sewn into its hem. She snipped the thread with nail scissors.

It was the ring. Bonnie tore all of the remaining clothes off their hangers and felt their hems. Sewn into a bed jacket was a pair of topaz cufflinks. In a pleated skirt was a gold locket on a chain. Bonnie started thinking about the other clothes—Hefty bags full of them—which over the last few months she had already brought to Goodwill.

The ring was platinum with a pear-shaped diamond and tiny emeralds on each side. I never saw the ring. I wish I had the ring. I relish the idea of Elva really having given it to me: singling me out as no one else has ever done, seeing some merit in my eyes, thinking—bolt from the blue—*I hardly know this girl and God knows whether she and Val will be together long, but something tells me she is very, very special.* And it would have meant so much to me, that some intrinsic spark meant more to her than flesh and blood, more than the crowded past. That was a daydream, though, built on the paranoia and proprietary instincts of poor bereaved Bonnie. Elva sewed her jewelry into hems—who did she wish would discover it there? Or did she misremember having told someone? Alive, we cling to our belongings or give them away, we cache and hoard them hatching fledgling plans and thinking secret thoughts. Alive, we make our choices, but dying, we forfeit, leaving the living to scatter, scramble, scratch, and outwit one another in their tussle to prove how much they were loved, how much we loved them, and what they are worth.

4.

isolation

THE HOSPITAL WHERE my father lay blubbering gibberish, stricken and out of his mind and incontinent and moored to machines by tubes and needles, had dazzling views of a lake ringed with trees whose names would make you want to laugh rather than cry: money tree, monkey puzzle, gum. Under the trees on weekdays were lovers in summer clothes, on weekends families picnicking and playing ball.

Dad jabbered in his bed and dozed and let my aunt and mother spoon his meals into his mouth. The blue skies and the lake outside looked like a holiday scene. He used to say I would regret leaving L.A., and he was right. I never told him he was, but he was.

In the hospital's air-conditioned basement, near what I think was the morgue, was a chapel where stained glass backlit by electric bulbs depicted lilies in green grass, a nonsectarian pastoral. Holy books from five faiths lined a table just inside the door, and you could pray for anything down there.

My friend Clark used to say that when *his* dad was dying in a hospital, his large family ate constantly. *It was a party*, Clark said—they were mourning, but hyped-up, manic with dread and impotence. The family laid out huge spreads in the waiting room. *My sister brought a chafing dish.* As if to cheat death however they could, show death that *some* folks were still in the pink, they ate and drank and rollicked, sort of. *I gained six pounds in a week*, Clark said.

That story always entertained me in a distant way, the way you are intrigued by strange tribes in anthropology books.

IT WAS NOT like that with us. We sat silent, starving and motionless for hours at a time. As night fell, gloom swallowed us in our chairs, the only light a yellow gleam spilling through the door from the hall. My father's catheter swelled fat and golden. My mother and aunt spoke, when they spoke at all, as if he were already dead. My aunt, calling her daughter in Ontario, said:

He's lying there, it's almost over now.

My mother called the cemetery. To confirm that a spot was reserved for him, thanks to good planning in happier times, as a spot was reserved for her.

He was jerking, his left side spastic. He seemed to be looking out the window at the trees but he was not. He could not—not without his glasses, which were deemed unsafe to wear given his seizures. Dad without his glasses, my aunt here at all—it was surreal, everything in the wrong place, like in a funny painting by Magritte in which a man's chest is a birdcage. If it was Monday, why was my father not at his office? Why was his hand refusing to hold a fork? It had held countless forks before, but now, even if you curled his fingers around the handle, they just fell open and the fork slid out. The way he acted, you would think there was *not* a nice slice of meat loaf and a bowl of choco-late pudding on his tray.

I walked the corridors. I went in out in out and back into his room. My thoughts fizzed, as if heard through an intercom. The doctors could not tell us whether he would live or die or stay sus-pended halfway in between. (Spoiler alert: he died.) One day I walked outside into the parking lot. The wind was menthol from the long-leaved gum trees whose bark was pliant and smooth, like skin. I saw a crushed bird on the concrete, a baby bird nearly bald but for black pinfeathers. Its black eye watched the sky, its beak unhinged. That was the only time I cried, and no one saw.

AFTER THE IMMUREMENT, which was not a funeral because there was a rabbi but no guests, five of us ate lunch in a cof-fee shop—the Parasol, whose golden roof was shaped like a huge umbrella. Over each table hung a lamp shaped like an umbrella, and the waitresses wore full skirts with umbrella ribs and spokes. My friend Patricia used to work there, and one night a man jumped out from behind the Dumpster and flashed her.

We took a booth. It was the sort of restaurant where tall slices of pie revolve in multi-tiered glass columns on the counter. Our wait-ress had no way of knowing we had been to an immurement. My aunt ordered liver and onions. I ordered a salad. A car dealership across the street was festooned with giant balloons and a sign that said EASY DEALS! The family friend who was doing the driving that day ordered a quesadilla and pronounced it *kwasadeel*. Mom ordered nothing. She was thinking of the house.

My father was out of context in the hospital, but at home, where he would have been *in* context, he was nowhere to be seen. Home was nothing *but* context. His clothes in the closet, his desk with its fossil paperweight, the sign on the door to his den that said CONFUCIUS SAY: GET THE @%*! OUT OF HERE. Context, context, everywhere you looked. So many things were so imbued with him in one way or another that touching whatever he had touched and then taking your hand away felt like betrayal. That first night it got to where even lifting one foot off the wall-to-wall carpet felt that way: betrayal, like good-bye, good-bye, good-bye.

A WEEK LATER I left my mother there. *You have to get back to your life*, she said.

And then I didn't talk about it.

My friend Doreen picked me up at the airport. All the way home she joked. She joked about the contractor who was fixing her house (*He has a harelip!*), and about a new Thai bar where all the hostesses were really men. She did not mention Dad, whom she had met a year before. I wondered whether she was trying to be nice, whether she might be waiting politely for me to start talking about him. But I did not talk about him; I could not. It did not fit into the conversation. It seemed inappropriate. After dropping me off, Doreen gave me a friendly wave.

At the office the next day, they all knew where I had spent the last three weeks and why, but no one mentioned it directly.

Only two out of three dozen co-workers mentioned it at all. One editor leaned close and whispered in my ear, *It's bad, right? Time helps.* Another hugged me—awkwardly, because she was the intern and we had never exchanged a word. Our receptionist, Daisy, asked how my mother was—because she was a woman of the same age. No one else said anything. A few gave me a nod and went about their tasks. I wondered vaguely if they should have bought me flowers, pitched in for them. Flowers were for sale at the liquor store down the street. I wondered whether it was rude that they had not.

They said nothing, I said nothing. A week later there was a cocktail party. Then a month later another one. By that time it was arguably too late for condolences, but none came anyway.

If you had seen me in those days, you never would have known this most salient fact about me. The ancient Scythians slashed their noses and ears and stabbed their hands with arrows to show that they were in mourning. These days we do not. No one passing us in the supermarket aisle has a clue.

ISOLATION SETS IN. Silence sets in. In the wake of a loss, it settles around you all thick and soft like a down comforter, like clouds outside an airplane window, like pudding and mashed potatoes, like white noise on TV and like sleep. My friend Jamie had moved to a new city and was working as an intern at a magazine office just a few weeks before his father died. His father had remarried years before, so it fell to Jamie to call his mother and tell her that her ex-husband was gone. That felt strange. *Then*, he says, *there was a void.* He had started his internship knowing that his father would die soon, but he hadn't yet made any close friends at the office with whom he could share the experience. When he took a few days off to attend the memorial service, a few of them were aware of the reason for his absence, but upon his return no one spoke of it. Now he saw the wide circle of his acquaintances as being divided into two camps: his old close friends, all of whom were on the opposite coast, and his co-workers at the office, whom he saw every day but barely knew. He became a silent, cryptic figure—hesitating to call his old friends, who might have talked him through it, because he didn't want to bug them. *You don't wanta be calling them up crying and go: Give me two hours of your time,* Jamie says now. *At work, they'd go, How are you? and I'd go, Fine, and that's it.* Maybe that was best, he reasoned. He didn't want to call attention to himself. Then he would be typecast in all their minds as *the intern whose dad just died.* Jamie reasoned that maybe it was best to just keep quiet, keep his mind off his pain and get a lot of work done. *But then that made me wonder: By keeping busy am I dishonoring myself? Am I dishonoring my father? Am I not being forthright with my colleagues?* He even had a new girlfriend—but the relationship was so new, and the young woman was so unmarked by loss in her own life, *that she wasn't really ready to deal with what was happening with me. We weren't close enough to have a vocabulary for that,* Jamie says.

Going about his daily routine, he wondered if others could see his anguish in his eyes. He suspected that they could, that they must, that even in his quiet comings and goings he must be giving off at least some hint of desperation, some bodily clue that could be translated as *help me.* If so, no one in his new life made that translation and Jamie would not pick up the phone to demand solace from his old life. He saw it that way—that time was marching on, that we are expected to move forward, not back.

Months later, he drove cross-country to visit his stepmother. She had kept his father's clothes all that time but now she offered them to Jamie. He was sorting through the items, choosing his favorites, when he discovered a shirt that he had given his father as a Christmas present a few years earlier. He remembered buying the shirt, feeling then that it suited the old man's taste perfectly—he could picture his father wearing it. Removing it from the closet now, he saw that it had obviously never been worn. The original shop tag was still on it. Jamie went cold all over. *He didn't even want it, and there I was, being asked to take it back.* Jamie wanted the shirt back, wanted to clutch it to his chest, but then again he didn't. It was a brand-new kind of insult that he had never felt before. It was an offense that held the key to a door Jamie didn't want opened, beyond which lay the discomfiting suspicion *that on some level I just didn't understand the man.* He was a nearly thirty-year-old son mourning a father he believed he knew. But now the doubts barraged him. To what extent was Jamie mourning a total stranger? In which case, to what extent was his mourning a sham? The unworn shirt, a pristine testament to false presumptions and to parts of lives unseen, to unbridged gaps that Jamie had not even known were there, raised questions he could hardly broach with himself, much less with others. No way could he fit those questions into an answer to *How are you?*

IT TOOK MY other friend, Justin, seventeen years to broach the subject of his father's death with friends. Even then he didn't come right out and say it. He had to write about it first, and publish his story in a newspaper.

The morning he woke up to discover the body of his father in the bunk bed they shared, Justin was eleven. The news saturated the neighborhood within a day. It was not a suspicious death or a violent one. It was a heart attack. But it was a death, and that was all it took to lay a stigma over Justin and his sisters.

It was as if our house had been painted black, he says. Mothers warned their sons to treat Justin gently. This is not the sort of advice that preteen boys always know how to handle. *Whenever I went out to play, every single kid was reacting to me weirdly. They were being super-nice and it was so obvious why.* It didn't comfort him. It made him feel paranoid that everyone was talking behind his back, that his friends were either handling him with kid gloves or completely avoiding him. *It got so bad that I just wished nobody even knew my dad had died.* When Justin started middle school a year later, he was relieved to find himself among strangers. With new friends, he kept the story of his dad a secret. Whenever the topic of fathers came up, he acted vague until the moment passed.

By the time he reached high school, not talking about his dad, and not thinking about his death any more than he could help it, were second nature for Justin. *Years and years of repeating to myself the fact that I didn't want to talk about it made me believe that I really didn't.* Sometimes a film in which a father died would catch him by surprise. *I would feel myself well up. But those were the only times*, he says.

He was twenty-eight and a newspaper staff writer and Father's Day was approaching when he realized that *after all those years of not wanting it to come up and praying that it wouldn't come up, I really wanted it to come up.* The story he wrote was intensely personal—describing the kind, handsome heavy smoker he remembered, recounting the death and its aftermath, and exploring Justin's own passion for cigarettes, a vice he had adopted at fourteen knowing full well that it had killed his dad.

Once a writer turns in a story for publication, it becomes public. *When that story ran,* Justin remembers, *I had this day or two of walking around feeling like my wiener was out. I felt so exposed.* But then co-workers started coming up to him wanting to talk—*not so much about my story but about the deaths of their own fathers, or some other death.* Within a few weeks, Justin felt as if he had grown up. *I could laugh and be wry about it. I could talk about his faults without blaming him. I could laugh at him. I could laugh at myself. I could talk about it in the context of a conversation without having to feel that it was off-limits. I didn't need to feel like I had any more secrets. But I can't believe it took that long,* he says. *I can't believe it took that many years.*

IN MODERN TIMES, in public places, you cannot as a rule distinguish mourners from celebrants or anyone else. The wearing of black—or white, the Chinese mourning color—is no indicator anymore. Some of the happiest people on any street are clad in black or white. Living in a crowded world of mixed societies, surrounded nearly all the time by total strangers, we have learned to blend into the scenery and not attract undue attention to ourselves. Living, too, in a clean culture that exalts prettiness and happiness and youth, one hesitates to inject ugliness into the picture. One is reluctant to bum folks out. If others cannot tell by looking at you that condolences are called for, they will hardly volunteer. They cannot read your mind. They cannot be expected to broach dire topics out of thin air. Why should they, if you seem unconcerned and offer them no clues? Gliding around in your see-through, portable cone of silence feeling resentful, feeling entitled, are you any different from the spoiled brat sulking at Christmas because Santa brought all the wrong gifts?

My best and oldest friend Jeannette lived six hundred miles away from me and we spoke seldom. When I called to tell her the news, her husband answered. Although he did not know my father, he knew *of* him and, handing the phone to his wife, said in a breaking voice, *He's dead!* That meant a lot somehow. They sent a cheese basket. But it was odd how those whom I saw nearly every day continued not to mention Dad, or death, or funerals. Is *How are you?* shorthand for all of that? Years later, one friend confessed that she could not speak of it because it seemed "too close to home," that if she broached the subject of *my* father and his fate, it might bring some misfortune down upon *her* father by the force of magic or the evil eye or irony. As if things worked that way, as if what I had were contagious.

During phone calls in those days, I often jerked the receiver from my ear and held it at arm's length, glaring at it as familiar voices chortled out, *tra-la-la-la* and never mentioned him. It was like that part of Groucho Marx's TV show in which he waited for a guest to say the daily secret word by chance, a funny word such as *kneecap* or *bulb*, and when it happened a toy duck on a swing emerged from the ceiling and the guest won a prize. I was making a list of whom never to forgive. They did not know this then. They do not know it yet. It was a game in which I would not talk but wanted, upon penalty of deep unspoken loathing, to be asked.

BUT WHAT WAS there to say? Death is ineffable. "There is no grief like the grief which does not speak," Longfellow wrote. Speaking to strangers of a man who died but whom they never knew can feel so silly, forced, theatrical, like being a child at show-and-tell, holding a rawhide bone, spluttering, *My dog Jingles is big.* Spectators humor you with nods and clucks. You leave feeling the fool.

Speaking of him to anyone who knew him, your mother for instance—what's the point? You hardly need to say, *He was so good at gardening!* You hardly need to jog each other's memories in order to remember or properly feel the blow of what is lost. She knows. You know she knows. Making proclamations about the dead means having to hear your voice strain to sum up, summarize, translate. Translating a life into words flattens it, coarsens it, like all translations. When the life is gone and only words are left, use them at your own risk.

At times like that, your voice is not up to the task and resembles a car backfiring or the braying of a mule. At times like that, talking becomes a brute bodily function not unlike sneezing, or gas.

Others urge us to get things off our chests, to share. Most of the time they are merely being polite. Anyway, how do you share a death? What aspect of it should you share? *Here—try this part.* A death is so big, as big as a galaxy, that breaking off bits of it here and there to parcel out would not be worth your while. When you are finished, most of it will still be left.

You might argue that sharing—speaking of the dead—honors the dead and in some way keeps them alive. You might say there is honor in broadcasting memories of him or her, flying his or her flag. You might say that if Otto Frank had kept his daughter's diary all to himself, Anne would be long forgotten now. She would be *really* dead and gone. But most of those who live are not like Anne, and most of those who die, die ordinarily. In the plain story of a plain man who wore plain blue suits, ate plain food, lived in a plain house in a plain town and died of a plain stroke, what could possibly spur a listener? It is not the story of Calvary, it is not *Braveheart.* Constrained to tell the plain story of a plain man, you might find yourself embroidering the facts, or rushing through it—by which you betray him all over again.

SOMETIMES WE ALSO hesitate to speak of the dead in order not to speak ill of them. We know a lot more than our listeners and those who send the Hallmark cards about this person who is gone. We know the nuanced truth. Typical words of sympathy are whitewashes—sometimes it almost makes you laugh. What if right in the middle of a hug from a well-wisher who said, *Sorry to hear the news,* you said, *It was good news!* Or just that your father was mean, or cheap, or liked to play cruel jokes, or called you Tubby. We are often angry at the dead. We were furious at them for many years before they died, or we are angry now because they died, or both. Who knows what might pop out of our mouths when they are not here to answer back? My father used to make fun of me when I cried. He said I wept too easily, and over stupid things, and he would mimic my mouth with his or mime playing a violin. *I'll give you something*, he would sneer, *to cry about*, and quite often he did. Telling the details would have meant revenge, but it would have also meant reveling in the presence of outsiders, which felt obscene.

Telling is giving. Giving is *giving away*. I was the keeper of the power of his death and all that my father had been. And words are pearls before swine. Cheaper than that. Words are little plastic beads.

Among the Warramunga of central Australia, visiting scholars in the late nineteenth century discovered that female mourners customarily took long vows of silence. Women closely related to the dead cut their hair after the funeral, daubed their bodies with clay, and for up to two years were allowed to communicate with others by sign language only.

That makes it easier in some ways. At least neither mourner nor well-wisher needs to grope, as we find ourselves doing now, for language to describe the indescribable. My friend Hope's mother committed suicide. It was a very deliberate act. She had made several previous attempts, and this one worked. Hope loved and missed her mother but was not surprised to sense a wall of silence descending between her and her friends. She was twenty, not an age when talking about death—*real* death, not death in movies or video games or fetishized in punk T-shirts—

comes naturally. Besides which, *suicide*, Hope says, *is the big taboo.* A depressed schoolmate had killed himself that year, which was discussed a bit among his peers, but somehow the suicide of a parent was such anathema, such an abomination as to be beyond imagination and thus beyond conversation. Hope knew better than to raise the subject. So she was touched at the unexpected arrival of a bouquet from a friend, along with a sympathy card. The friend had clearly labored over what to write inside the card. She settled on: *Sorry about what happened to your mother.*

Reading the card, Hope laughed out loud. She was touched, but she could not stop laughing. *Happened to your mother—like she broke her leg! It wasn't exactly an accident.*

THE SEASON AFTER my father died, someone I hardly knew had the job of dropping off deliveries on my porch every Friday evening—documents to be proofread over the weekend. One Friday not long after I came back from L.A., she left a pan of muffins by the door, on top of the manila envelope. There was no mawkish card. Just these, golden and firm. The next Friday I left the washed pan on the porch. I could have been there when she came. I could have sat out on the stairs waiting for her. Since she had made this overture, we could have had a talk. Instead I left a note on the empty pan. It said, Thank you. Leaving the pan and the note on the doormat I hurried to the farthest part of the house so that I would not hear her car pulling up outside. I did not want to talk. She rang the bell. From the darkness at the back of the house I pictured her standing out there, her long legs and sheaf of black curls. The doorbell echoed through the rooms, unanswered. The next Friday I sat in the dark again. She left a bag of oranges that time. She simply left it on the mat. She did not ring the bell that time. She was a saint for that.

5.

guilt

ENISE USED TO bounce down the hall in our dorm wearing earphones and carrying a radio—not a walkman, but an embarrassing old transistor in a red vinyl case with her name on it, in stick-on letters. Wearing acrylic sweaters and extra-long jeans—because she was six feet tall— patterned with faux patchwork, she was listening to ABBA, the Bee Gees, KC and the Sunshine Band, thin arms plying the air. She thought she was disco-dancing, but Denise had no idea how to disco-dance. No one had ever taught her how. Two girls down the hall, Jackie and Liz, had taught her the most laugh-able routine they could think of, all skip-hops and propeller arms, which they had invented on the spot but told Denise was a hot new dance sensation called the New York Scramble. She believed them—that was her all over, believing whatever she was told by girls with cute tube tops and feathered bangs. Skip-hopping down the hall, thin arms a blur, Denise sang right out loud with the music in her ears. *Ooooooh—love to love you baby!* And in every room—the doors always stood open—girls watched Denise go by and laughed. But Denise never saw them laughing at her, because the only way to do the New York Scramble was with eyes shut tight.

From the other girls she sought advice on fashion. *Tuck the bottoms of your jeans into your socks*, they told her. *Really! The models in Paris do it!* From the other girls she sought advice on love. *What?* they shrieked. *Never even kissed a guy? Well, someday you will but you have to know exactly how. Here, show us how you'd kiss a guy, come on, kiss this pillow.* The other girls taught her to smoke and right before the Fleetwood Mac concert, three of them gave Denise cocaine. They cut it into lines with a razor blade on a little mirror imprinted with a Coca-Cola logo that said "Coke." *I'm high!* she trilled. *I'm hiiiiigh.* She spent the concert jogging in place, at her seat. She stayed awake for twenty-four hours straight, washing and setting her hair three times and removing all the posters from her wall—Mikhail Baryshnikov, Robin Gibb, a worm perched atop an apple reading a book—and pinning them back up, in different positions, time after time until the coke wore off. From the other girls she sought advice on makeup. *More eye shadow, yes, thicker*, they told her, giggling, *more, here, try this green kind.* For everything else, and after she had been everywhere else, she came to me and Renée.

She loped into Renée's room and lay across the bottom bunk. Her feet dangled over the end rail; she was too tall for the dorm beds. *I loooove ABBA, you guys.* Her hip bones jutted through her patchwork jeans like fins. *I don't feel so well today.* She never felt well—as a child she had suffered near-fatal kidney infections and now had only one kidney. Her feet jiggled in time to songs she hummed. *Who on this hall do you think has had sex?* Denise would ask us. *Have they all had sex? I like a guy in my macroeconomics class. His name is Paul. I would have sex with him if he asked me. He never looks at me, no way is he ever going to ask me. But I would do it. Who do you guys wish would ask you to have sex? Will I be old before I have sex? Will I be old before I even get a date? My stomach hurts. You guys got any gum?* The difference between Renée and I and the other girls is that we told Denise the truth. Not that she knew this was the difference, but we did. The only thing we never told Denise was that she was a laughingstock. She never asked. We never said.

SHE ALWAYS SAT with us at meals. The other girls would never be seen with Denise in public. One night Renée was giving her a hard time. *Have something besides peas, for godsakes.*

Not hungry, Denise said and pushed her plate away. *I don't feel well.*

With a frown she dropped a cookie into her purse for later, just in case. Then Denise laid her tray on the conveyor belt and walked away.

We never saw her again. In the library that night, she died.

Students who were sitting nearby said they saw her turn blue, froth at the mouth, drop her pencil, and slide out of her chair onto the floor. One of them was a lifeguard and tried CPR.

ALL OF US from the dorm were summoned into the lounge by the resident assistant, a senior named Otto with a nervous laugh. *They have to do an autopsy but hee hee hee, the doctor at the Health*

Center said it looked like a heart attack. I know this is a hee hee hee, big shock for all of you.

The weirdest thing happened then. The other girls began to cry.

Andrea, one of the three who'd given Denise cocaine, started it. Then Liz and Jackie who had invented the dance. It was contagious and the girls were falling all over each other, screaming softly, sprawling on the carpet and beating it with their fists. The sounds of sobs and screams mixed with the chime of the clock tower in the plaza. Across the room the boys from downstairs sat in stony silence, looking at their feet.

I waited to cry, but nothing came. Renée and I sat like wooden statues, holding hands.

That night we lay in the dark listening to disco, saying nothing but laughing now and then like Otto. From all up and down the hall you could hear screams and sobs. Someone was in the bathroom shouting.

We were told we could attend a family memorial service at Denise's home in Burbank, a two-hour drive. Without asking, Jackie and Liz climbed into the backseat of Renée's car. *Let's go to Denise's thing.* They wore wraparound skirts and halter tops. They flicked their hair. We started down the highway past the lemon groves. *Play Joni,* Jackie said, jerking a thumb at the box of cassettes. *I love Joni. Or David Bowie if you have him.* That bitch. She never liked disco really. In the backseat Liz crossed and uncrossed her legs. Her rayon skirt made a skeechy sound.

Renée popped in a Shaun Cassidy tape. *Hey, Deanie, won't you come out tonight? The summer's waitin' and the moon is shinin' so bright.*

Hey, Deanie, you're the one I'm dreamin' of. That's when Renée cried, and so did I.

When we reached the house, Liz and Jackie climbed out and ran with their arms waving in the air to the woman who could only be Denise's mother, the woman standing at the front door with streaks through her pancake makeup. *We came from the schoooool.* They flung themselves on her. *Ohhhh Deniiiiise.*

WHEN YOU TORMENT others while they are alive, the last thing you imagine is that they might die before you can ask them for forgiveness, before you get a chance to confess your crimes or disappear into the distant past. You've done whatever harm it was, and justified it who knows how – because it seemed hilarious at the time, because you saw your chance, because you thought your victim was asking for it. Maybe you only did it once. Maybe you only did it twice. Maybe it was a lifestyle choice. Remember all the lies you told your little sister: *Those metal slots in the floor? Why, that's another kind of toilet.* Then you ran and tattled: *Mom! Dad! Kylie pissed into the heating vents!* You laughed. Who could resist? That was water under the bridge, you tell yourself. Time flies. And then she dies.

And death transfixes cruelty. Death snatches away all chances to apologize, time's chance to heal all wounds. Death transforms past behavior from a fluid—which could be changed or diluted or flushed away—into a solid, as surely as gelatin sets a mold. And even though death seems a blessing for tormentors whose victims take all their secrets to the grave, guilt niggles and guilt overwhelms. Your deeds haunt you, and every step feels like the New York Scramble.

In a famous Kabuki play, an attractive young woman named Oiwa has a faithless husband who feeds her a dose of "road blood medicine"—a poison that disfigures before it kills. Oiwa goes bald, one of her eyes seals itself shut, the other eye becomes fixed in a grotesque position, with its iris staring starkly upward. She dies filled with hatred for her husband, who now feels free to enact his plan of marrying a beautiful neighbor. On his wedding day, he lifts the veil to see not his new bride but the hideous Oiwa. From that day forward, her distorted face appears everywhere, superimposed over live human faces, over paper lanterns, mingled with the smoke rising from fires. The guilt-wracked man strives vainly for absolution and finds none.

If regret is the agony of what you did not do, guilt is the agony of what you did.

I HEARD THIS story about the friend of a friend: She was a thirty-something woman whose husband had affairs with other women right under her nose. Moreover, he treated her as if she were a household servant. This couple had two children—precocious preteens who, taking their cues from their father, refused to lift a finger around the house and taunted their mother with wordplay that she could barely understand, because they teased in English and English was not her first language. After years of hearing this benighted creature describe her life, one day my friend was horrified to learn that the wife and mother had become very sick and was not expected to live out the year.

But it's the most amazing thing, my friend's dying friend marveled, her voice cracking with gratitude. *Jay and the kids are being wonderful to me.*

She called it a 180-degree turnaround, and I could picture it all: the gentle solicitude, the somber gazes, the plumped pillows, the glasses of water, the soft words and tender caresses. And I wanted to ask that man and his kids: whose soul are you striving to put at rest, you creeps?

And will you weep like willows at her funeral? You will. You hope observers who did not know the truth will never learn your dirty secrets. You hope those who knew will keep their mouths shut or that, better yet, based on your tears, they will say they misjudged you. Already you are hustling to rewrite the past. *Our darling mother!* It is in your hands now, as the dead can neither write nor speak. For the eyes of the world you are writing a narrative of how you wish it was, or how you wish it would be seen. A revisionist history.

My ex-roommate Meadow was sixteen when she stopped talking to her father and he stopped talking to her. If you had asked Meadow why, as I asked her, she would have shrugged and said, *Just 'cuz he's an asshole.* Before they stopped talking, they fought often. Meadow wanted private singing lessons for which he refused to pay. To his face Meadow called him low-class, mocked his sleeveless undershirts and ridiculed the foods he liked, Moon Pies and Cheez-Its. Meadow had dyslexia and was slower in school than her elder sister. Her father made no secret of his preference for the sister. He came out and said so all the time. Once at a family barbecue to which she invited me, I overheard a friend remarking to him that Meadow looked cute in her outfit that day. Meadow was nearly thirty then. It was a red cowgirl jacket with a matching miniskirt. He sipped his 7-Up and, watching both daughters across the lawn, said, *I prefer the other one.* Just like that. Later at the party, Meadow talked about her father right in front of him. *Can you believe how fat he looks? It comes from watching* Love Boat *reruns all day. Lazy ass.*

Diabetes made him weak and mainly prone, his last two years. In that time Meadow dropped by occasionally to visit her mother, who was caring for him. On those visits Meadow would address her mother over the bed or couch where her father lay, as if he weren't there. Then she would leave without saying good-bye.

And then he died.

She called me that night. *My daaaad died.* It was as if she were speaking about a different father in a different time. Meadow had not called him "my dad" in years. She used to call him "him." Now she talked of his final day in detail, as you would about someone you loved. *Then he asked my mom for another glass of water. Then he had a headache. Then he felt dizzy and saw stars when he tried to sit up. Then he watched* Dynasty *and fell asleep. Then he—*

She and her sister were planning the funeral.

We're going to write the ceremony, Meadow said. But what kind of consensus could they find? I pictured Meadow's sister in the chapel praising the old man's kindness and cheer as Meadow, by her side, shrieked, *He ate Cheez-Its!*

But the service was all praise. *My daaaad*, Meadow began, and might as well have been delivering a eulogy for Santa Claus, or Martin Luther King. *My daaaad*. At the podium, Meadow and her sister took turns making proclamations beginning like that. When they were done, they fell upon each other wailing. Everyone watched Meadow cry. You never heard such loud crying. Some of them knew and some did not.

Sobbing, she looked back and saw the years and years of silence, a twelve years' war from which she was limping away on cut feet, tattered, burned, and shell-shocked. Sobbing, Meadow knew it was her fault, that she had started this war, she, not he, although he had grabbed the gauntlet gladly enough. Sobbing while row on row of friends, neighbors, and relatives regarded her with open curiosity, she wondered if it had all been really necessary, could she have said something, sometime, even just once to break it, but she knew right there and then that no, she could not and would never have. She sobbed for guilt. She also sobbed for her incredibly bad luck: of all the fathers in history, in the wide world, she had to get him. Could any other father have provoked her as he did? Could any other human being have so winkled out the worst in her? She sobbed for fate and for the fact that it was over now, the stupid confluence of genealogy and personality that drove her to this point. She dug the heels of her hands into her slippery cheeks. And she would never have another father, she would never love a father, she would never have that chance.

SOME PEOPLE NEVER seem to feel guilty about anything and some of us feel guilty about everything. We skulk shamefacedly in sunny flower fields or while accepting pay raises or unwrapping our birthday gifts. We smirk at every compliment as if it were a joke, lest it make us sound better than we really are. Even on happy days we hesitate to say, *Everything's fine!* because what if, for some reason yet to be revealed, it is not?

I WOULD LIKE to assert that I never tormented anyone the way Liz and Jackie in the dorm tormented Denise. I would like to declare that nothing I have done to anyone merits inclusion in this chapter. I would like to say that no matter who dies now, my hands are clean. But is it true? Of course not. I did things. I made up nicknames for others: The Human Fish. Big Chief White-ass. Spot. I called a girl named Patti Addams Panty Addumbs. Other crimes: Gossip. Sabotage. Duplicity, oh yeah. Sneaking away. What is the punishment for giving praise while laughing silently inside—then, later, shrieking gleefully: *He actually thought it was good!*

Whether or not a victim knows he or she is a victim hardly matters. Denise never knew that Liz and Jackie—lithe and supple in their leotards and cutoffs—were tormenting her. She thought they were her friends. Pathetic.

Other victims *know.* Was I only thirteen when the boy everyone made fun of liked me and I let him? He blurted out declarations I wanted to hear, though not from him, bought me a copper ring and shamed himself by shouting red-faced in the crowded quad at lunchtime: *Why get high on drugs? The true high is TRUE LOVE!* Was I only nineteen that summer I spent in the Rockies not calling or writing to my boyfriend? We had been

dating for two years. It was just a summer job. We had not broken up. We were not planning to break up. Everything was fine.
I left Los Angeles that June amid promises and plans. He too
gave me a ring: a pearl, from a shop on the esplanade that let
customers pick their own live oysters out of a tank. Then in the
pines beside the lake whose white swans, said the park rangers,
mate for life, I could neither bring myself to write him nor to call.
I mean I *could* have, physically. There *was* a phone. I called my
parents on it. On beige hotel stationery with its pointy-mountain
logo I wrote to my friend Jeannette. But that boy back home by
the sea, learning to play a bass guitar, became abstract, a paper
cutout on which no one had penciled a face. He agonized. Had
he been free, had he known he was free, he could have cruised
in his Ford Pinto and scored chicks. But no. His letters arrived
daily, his script spikier in every one. *Are you still mine? Or is there
someone else?* I was not. There was not. He went to see my dad
and begged him to beg me.

I tried to justify it to myself. In the big hotel kitchen, washing plates rimed with trout skin and beef stew, I would remind
myself of that boy's little jibes, the times he slagged Jeannette,
the way he liked to say, like a philosopher, *Some girls are beautiful
and some are cute and you are cute.* I told myself that he had brought
his punishment upon himself.

I heard recently that he is married now with two kids. Alive.
So you might say he turned out well in spite of that summer. In
spite of me. You might say I was easy to forget. You might say
I am blameless after all. You might say: that summer, so what?
But while it lasted, I tortured that boy. He lives, OK, but were

he dead, I would wonder: among his days, that finite number totaled up and gone, how many were wasted on me?

No matter who dies, no matter if it happens miles away from us, no matter if we are not there and have no reason to be there and it is officially an accident or natural causes, we guilty types will find some way to say, *It was my fault.* Ditto if the death was long in coming and no surprise to anyone. No matter what, we will call ourselves murderers. Then the self-loathing we have always felt makes perfect sense. If something bad has happened, somewhere, to someone, we *must* have had something to do with it. It all seems connected, our loathsomeness, our fault. It is a childish impulse, narcissistic in the way that toddlers generate gravitational fields around themselves, in which everything that happens is *all about me!* How selfish of us to impose our free-floating guilt on another's death. It muddles the true story, dishonors the dying.

I know a woman whose husband died young of a heart attack while making love with her. She felt guilty. She had known for years about his weak heart, and for years after his death her own arousal terrified her, because she was convinced that she was a sexual monster whose relentless demands had mown down a helpless man. I know another woman whose husband also died young, also of a heart attack, also while making love—but not with her. They had separated, with plans to divorce, and he was with someone he barely knew. His wife anguished, telling herself that had she not initiated the breakup, he would have survived because he would have suffered the attack while having sex with her—*and I would have known where to find his nitroglycerin.*

You run and rerun the sequence that led to the death over and over in your mind, or out loud to whoever seems willing to sympathize. All this revising casts you as a villain now enlightened; as a prisoner sentenced to the endless recitation of his crime; as a helpless victim of time. Your script becomes psalmic. It transforms you into the Ancient Mariner, who in the poem by Coleridge is doomed to roam the land accosting strangers and forcing them to hear his narrative about killing a lucky albatross and thus bringing misfortune upon his ship and its crew. "Unhand me, graybeard loon!" shouts a youth who does not want to stop and hear the tale, but is unable to escape.

Like the mariner, you seek forgiveness, absolution, penance everywhere, from everyone but those who could have granted it. Two hundred sailors on that ship, the old man says, *all dead did lie:*

> *And a thousand thousand slimy things*
> *Lived on; and so did I.*

And sometimes you feel guilty just for being alive. We are not meant to take the phrase *dodging a bullet* literally. Laughing or shuddering, we use those words to denote any near miss. But now and then it's real. Someone dies in your stead. Someone was where you were (or where you meant to be), doing what you did (or were meant to do), and by some magnitude of chance (long shot or close call), you escaped unscathed and someone else, just one flick of the wrist away, did not.

Dodging a bullet is a rite of passage, an initiation, a troth—because, henceforth, you will forever know that you were spared, and wonder why. You will be grateful for this gift, the precious gift of life. But it is perverse gratitude. It's tainted. You know you should be glad to be alive, but then again you feel as if you shouldn't be, because this kind of gladness translates into: *I'm glad it wasn't me*, which then translates into *I'm glad it was him*. The first reflex is thankfulness, the kind that makes you cross yourself or swear a vow or kiss the ground. Yet your euphoria is spiked with nausea. Since *someone* caught the bullet that you missed, counting your blessings just seems mean.

Were you spared so that you can *do* something? But what? Then does this mean that those who died *instead of you* were destined to achieve nothing at all? Were all their ambitions illusory, absurd? A co-worker of mine died in his sleep of respiratory failure last year at the age of twenty-nine. Just two months earlier he had graduated from journalism school. It seemed a brutal irony, all that homework he did, those days in class: the fun he missed. Was he actually *never meant to be a journalist*? In which case, remaining alive and sitting at a cubicle just down the hall from his, must I write all the better because Isaac can't? The fact of his death, this young man so newly hired that outside the office I never would have recognized him, preys upon my mind. Not that he died so I could live, of course. Who would believe that? But still. Was his lost chance *my* chance?

RAY CHARLES WAS not born blind. He still had his eyesight at age six when he helplessly watched his younger brother George drown in a freak washtub accident. Nine months after the accident, Charles lost his eyesight to glaucoma. His biographers suggest that Charles perceived his blindness as a form of punishment, and that his guilt over George drove him to begin using heroin as a young man. In the film *Ordinary People*, based on the novel by Judith Guest, two young brothers are out in a boat when it capsizes. Conrad and Buck struggle to stay afloat, but Buck loses his grip on the overturned vessel and drowns. Conrad survives. His guilt—at having somehow been stronger and luckier, at not having been able to hold his brother's head above water—is exacerbated by his mother's thinly veiled certainty that the wrong son was saved.

SOME DODGED BULLETS are not metaphors. When he was fourteen, my ex-boyfriend Reed used to hang out at the house where his big sister Dawn lived with her boyfriend, Roscoe. It was a rambling house without much for a kid to do except listen to records and fold little cutout paper squares into the parcels in which Dawn and Roscoe sold cocaine. Reed had deft fingers and could fold for hours at a stretch.

A stream of customers was always pouring through the house, four or five at a time. Some waited on the sofa in the living room while one at a time went with Dawn and Roscoe into a back room. In the course of a week, tens of thousands of dollars would change hands. Not trusting banks, Roscoe and Dawn usually cached their savings in coffee cans, but sometimes in the rush a wad of bills would wind up stuffed under a pillow or inside a book, to be retrieved later, or not.

One day, Reed was in the living room choosing a record to play. Dawn had a huge collection of Led Zeppelin bootlegs.

With him was a man called Sly, a customer who liked to hang around the house and thought of Dawn as his best friend. Sly was fat and had a job and teenage kids of his own and he was always cordial to Reed. They were looking at a record jacket when Roscoe rushed in.

Where's the money? he howled. His eyes were wide and wild, the way they got sometimes, and sweat darkened the armpits of his shirt. Years of drug use had damaged Roscoe's ability to think clearly. He sometimes lapsed into bouts of paranoia. But this was the worst yet.

Sly sat up on his heels. *The what?*

Money, you motherfucker.

A pile of money was missing. Roscoe thought it was between seven and eight thousand dollars and he was sure he had stashed it in a hat. From the last time he saw it until that moment, no one had been in the house but himself, Sly, and Reed.

Which one of you motherfuckers has it? 'Cuz I ain't got time for this.

Not me, man. Sly shrugged and his belly jumped. *I wouldn't rip you off.*

Me, neither, Reed said, wincing to hear his voice come out so shrill. He never took money from the house, no matter what, because despite his unorthodox upbringing he had a firm moral compass that defined stealing as wrong.

Bullshit! I said gimme back my fuckin' money!

Dude, said Sly. *I told ya—*

He looked up in time to see Roscoe whip a gun from behind his back.

You motherfuckers.

The gun was a shiny steel revolver. It was the first gun Reed
had ever seen up close. Its barrel swung in an arc back and
forth between the fat man and the boy, pointing at Sly, then
Reed, then Sly, then Reed, pointing at their foreheads, then
their hearts.

Now look, said Sly in a low steady voice, *I said—*

Roscoe fixed the gun on him.

Strip.

What?

Strip! You got that money on you somewhere if you got it, fatty.

Sly lowered his hands slowly and began unzipping his pants.
They slipped around his ankles and he stepped out of his shoes.
He pulled his shirt over his head with the deliberateness of a
mime. His belly heaved.

You see, man? Zilcho.

*Take off everything. You could have it stuffed down your damn
underwear.*

Sly shifted uncomfortably. *Not in front of the kid, man.*

OK, do it in here. Roscoe waved the gun toward a bedroom.
Sly, arms half raised, stepped sideways through the door. Roscoe followed him.

Reed unexpectedly found himself alone. In a matter of seconds he slid open a window and crawled out onto the porch.
And then he was gone. The sound of his sneakers hitting the
pavement was the only sound he heard.

That night his mother told him Roscoe was in jail. *He shot
someone, a friend of Dawn's.* Dawn had arrived home that night to
find Roscoe rocking on his heels beside the bed and Sly dead,

the shag carpet stiff with his blood. She told Roscoe that she had found his pile of money—it was $6,200—in the hat before she left the house that day and put it somewhere safer, wedged under the loose bracket that held one of the legs of the dining-room table. She had meant to tell Roscoe before she left, but she forgot.

His mother was still saying something but Reed was not listening anymore. His knees were shaking. He sat down and started shaking all over. He thought: Whatever happens to me, *ever*, from now on is extra. Bonus. Whatever happens from now on is what I should be thankful for and what I almost didn't get.

He thought of Sly and the shaking got worse. *Not in front of the kid.* And even then, even at fourteen —*that* close to not making it to fifteen—Reed thought: At least I didn't love him. At least Sly was not my brother or my father or my friend because, if he were, what would I be thankful for? What would feeling glad to be alive feel like then?

Sigmund Freud was thinking of a kind of guilt when he devised the term *reaction formation* to describe a defense mechanism by which we behave in the exact opposite direction from our true emotions. We do this, Freud deduced, out of fear that our emotions are socially unacceptable and that, if we were to act on them, they might have appalling consequences. A classic example of this mechanism would be a compulsively scrupulous housewife who scrubs every surface in her home to a high polish, keeps vigilant watch over her children and feels their foreheads constantly for signs of fever: a woman who, before setting the family's dinner on the table, inspects it for shards of broken glass. Under analysis, this supermom is revealed to harbor deep resentment and murderous rage toward her husband and children. Subconsciously—as Freud would have it—she fears that if left to her own devices she might resort to murder, either by violence or by some less detectable method, such as poisoning. Horrified, she creates a reaction formation, burying in compulsive housekeeping her guilt for deaths that she is struggling subconsciously not to cause.

When someone *does* die, it works in reverse. Do you speak extra-nicely of the dead to overcompensate for how you spoke of them, or to them, when they were still alive? After the poet Percy Bysshe Shelley drowned in a boating accident, his widow Mary Wollstonecraft Shelley devoted herself to exalting his memory and glorifying his image. She was driven at least in part by guilt over the fights she had picked with him, often in public, in the weeks before his death: he had loved the Italian retreat to which they had come from England, calling it "this divine bay," while she wrote pettishly to a friend that she would feel no less miserable "had we been wrecked on an isle of the South Seas." Her guilt was deepened by the attitude of his friends, who showed whose side they were on by refusing to vouchsafe her any of the relics they had collected at the scene of his cremation, which she could not attend. Two friends seized pieces of Shelley's jawbone, another what remained of his heart. In fact Shelley had not always been kind to his young wife, and their fights were not always her fault: no matter, though, because her guilt convinced her otherwise.

. . .

AT THE MEMORIAL service in Burbank, Denise's mother embraced Jackie and Liz in the hallway as Renée and I loitered behind them in the foyer, next to a plaster replica of Rodin's *Thinker*. At the far end of the hall, in the living room, other guests were making their way to folding chairs arranged in rows. A light classical record was playing. Back in the dorm before she died, Denise used to tell us about her family a lot. Her father was passive and sweet and she loved him; he ran a flooring business. Her mother was sharp and had been beautiful and now took Valium and said Denise could attract a boyfriend if only she weren't so tall. Denise's brother was a junior at UCLA who wanted to someday own a tennis club.

I tried to remember more of this as Denise's mother called to her husband, who was in the living room. *Richard*, she trilled. *These are the girls—from the school.* He glanced up with a dazed half-smile, clearly in shock, a stack of mimeographed programs in one hand, his thin hair mussed and his free hand over his belly, looking like a baker in a nursery rhyme. *Denise's frieeeends*, her mother said. *See? She really had friends!* Holding Jackie and Liz by the hands, she led us all into a room off the hallway which I recognized at once as having been Denise's, with its orange carpet and matching wallpaper with a circus-animals design.

I want—to give you something.

Denise's mother made her way unsteadily on high-heeled sandals across the rug. If you did not know the reason, you would have thought she was crying and walking that way because she was drunk. Black-and-tan streaks of melted eyeliner and foundation sluiced all the way down her neck. On Denise's dresser was a padded-satin jewelry box which, when flicked open, revealed a tiny plastic ballerina inside, twirling mechanically to the tune of "Raindrops Keep Fallin' on My Head." Inside the box were two chokers, one a copper chain with a sun-shaped pendant and the other white macramé with shells. Denise's mother lifted them out, one in each hand, like offerings at a rite.

These belonged to my girl.

At the sound of that, Jackie and Liz leaned into one another and howled, tipping their heads back.

Deniiiise! Their hair swung as they wept. *Deniiiise!* They clasped their faces with wet fingers. Denise's brother was now standing in the doorway, wearing shorts and a rugby shirt, balding already, with a mustache.

I want you to have these. She would have wanted me to give you these.

They fastened the chokers around each other's necks. *Ohmigod, ohmigod thank you soooo much, this is soooo sweet.* It was difficult for them to see the clasps through their tears.

Her friends! Denise's mother said, biting her fist.

Renée slouched alongside Denise's closet, her broad shoulders slack under her blazer.

The service was starting in the living room. Of this I can remember nothing. Afterward we drank red punch and said good-bye. *You have a long drive back*, Denise's brother said, walking the four of us out to the car. *Welp, thanks for being here.* He threw an arm around Jackie and kissed her.

On the lips! she shrieked as we were turning the corner. *He put his tongue in!*

[GUILT]

We were halfway to the lemon groves when Liz unclasped
her choker.

Trade you, she said to Jackie and dangled it. They laughed.
These are so dumb.

6.

apathy

SOMETIMES YOU FEEL nothing at all.

Not sad. Not glad. Not even numb-because-you-are-in-shock. Not confused. Not sorting things out. Because there is nothing to sort out, nothing being the operative word.

It seems so simple, nothingness. So clean, in a Zen sort of way. Yet feeling nothing after someone dies can be quite messy. Because you wonder, *Is that all there is?* and wonder whether you are incapable of feeling. You wonder whether you are a sociopath. But you are not, because you have feelings, you do, you feel things all the time, you felt something just yesterday. Just not about this death. Just not about this person who has died. It was someone close, someone to whose death you are expected to react, you really are. But you cannot. Which sends you staring backward down the years, rehashing. *Feel something*, you implore yourself, terrified, because this was someone you knew, or thought you knew, and who knew you. But you cannot. A life has ended and you sit as unmoved as a tumulus, which makes you ask, *Is this my fault or theirs?*

. . .

MY GRANDMOTHER WAS not the kind to cuddle or confide in
or the kind to call you nicknames such as Princess, Pussycat, or
Doll. She was not mean to me. My friend Jeannette once asked
me, Is your grandma strict like mine? and I said, Strict? Like
making rules and hitting you with sticks? and Jeannette said,
Exactly. I said no. My Nana never spoke harshly to me, but then
I did not require discipline. She never scolded me—though once
she told me not to touch a dog. This was a prophetic remark,
as things turned out. Nana was neither harsh nor sugary, but
distant, wrestling with her troubles. Once at Chanukah she
gave me a Cher record that, I later learned, had been chosen
by a Kmart clerk whom she had asked what twelve-year-old
girls like. She was restless. My grandfather was deaf in one
ear, senile, and walked with a strange Popeye gait, all of which
embarrassed her. She had followed my parents to Los Angeles
from New York but had made no friends. On Sundays when we
drove to her apartment, she would talk for hours about illnesses
she had or thought she might catch. Anemia, evinced by white
membrane instead of pink under the eye. Pleurisy. Shingles.
Boils—one day she showed us one, lifting her skirt hem to reveal
what resembled a tapioca pearl: *Not worth lancing, the doctor said,
that idiot.*

My grandfather exhaled cigar smoke. *Kill the Krauts!*

Nana grew angry with my parents when they took me on
vacation. *How can you go off like that and leave two old people alone?*
They were not shut-ins, though. My grandfather still drove a
yellow Falcon and played cards at a club down the street.

One weekend when I was fifteen it was decided that we would go to the desert, all of us. At the motel, Nana hung her shifts in the closet and rubbed Ben-Gay on her arms. The sun had leached all color from the wooden fence around the pool, where guests lolled on deck chairs like cutlets. We ate in the coffee shop and toured the town. The next day, Sunday, Nana was standing beside the pool when a fellow guest emerged from a room leading a dog. The dog was on a leash, but it broke free and raced toward Nana. Its owner clapped her hands and called the dog. *Socrates, no!* And Nana, scrambling to avoid the leash, tripped over it. Her left hip hit the concrete with a sound like peanut brittle breaking in a bag.

She refused to go to the desert hospital nearby, even though Bob Hope and Frank Sinatra always stayed there when they were ill. Instead she demanded to go by ambulance all the way back to Los Angeles. The drivers wouldn't let my mother ride in the ambulance. The three of us packed in a rush and raced down the freeway after it.

Off-ramps flicked past under a purpling sky. YUCCA LANE: 2 MILES. OASIS AVENUE: NEXT TWO EXITS. My mother was acting in a way I did not recognize, thumping her forehead with her fists. *I could have caught her! She was falling and I saw her start to fall and if I was faster I could have caught her!*

Stop it, said my father in the cold voice he used to control emergencies. *She went down too fast.* Headlights and taillights and stoplights flew past in the night, redwhitegreen like spumoni ice cream.

Shut up, she said.

Shut up, he said.

Jake ran off to France, said my grandfather, *with a hooker.*

Drive faster, my mother said.

This is the speed limit, my father said.

Exceed it then, she said.

And I was thinking, There goes our vacation. If she had not fallen we would be back there by the pool. We would have been deciding where to eat.

I watched the passengers in other cars. They seemed so calm, so happy. They were not driving to hospitals. I envied them. We passed a restaurant shaped like a wigwam whose sign said STEAKS SHAKES CAKES. I had never visited someone in a hospital. I pictured the cartoons on get-well cards, a chipmunk with a toothache, a sea urchin in love with a hypodermic needle, a fat person in traction. In my head I heard that old joke: *Doc, I broke my arm! Does that mean I will never play the violin?*

Of course you will!

Hooray! I never could before!

Towns flashed past. Houses, banks, schools. HOME OF THE WOLVERINES. I wondered whether the stores in those towns were good, whether the boys were cute. My grandfather broke wind.

She's going to die, my mother said.

No, said my father. *People break their hips and get them fixed these days, as good as new.*

The anesthetic, she said. *Sometimes on the operating table they have bad reactions to the anesthetic and they die.*

What a load of bullshit, he said, but I could see him wondering.

I thought about my room at home. I thought about my friend Jeannette. What was she doing right that minute? My mother was crying, pounding the dashboard softly with the heels of her hands. I wanted her to be all right. I wanted her to smile the way she had when we were driving on this same road in the opposite direction the day before. I wanted her to talk to my father in her regular voice, but he was hunched down and she was making a creepy noise. It struck me then, somewhere near Anaheim, that I was not thinking about Nana much at all.

I was not thinking about falling or about how cramped an ambulance must feel. I was not thinking about broken bones and what it means to *not be able to stand up*. I thought about it *then*, for a fleeting moment in the car, and only because I ordered myself to.

I tried to cheer them up. I said, *Nana will be all right*. My mother whipped around and bit my head off. *How the hell do YOU know?*

We were nearly there. *Nearly there*, I said, but no one said anything.

Nana survived the surgery. The day she was released, my mother was so grateful that she brought a box of cookies for the nurses—a big paper box of butter cookies frosted yellow with painted-on smiley faces. The nurses clustered around the box. It was not every day a patient's family brought them things. In a wheelchair, Nana steepled her fingers. *Can we get out of this hellhole now*, she said.

And I thought, Well! That was a close one, but it's over now.

· · ·

NANA AND PAPA moved into our guest room, which became the sickroom with its vials of pills and the walker with which Nana was supposed to do her exercises. A physical therapist came to our house to help her with these, but after the first visit Nana stopped getting out of bed. *Donwanna*, she said. *What for?* She would not even get up to go to the bathroom. She stopped eating, rejecting the pretty meals my mother brought her on a tray.

The doctors at the hospital had warned her against lying still. It was bad for the circulation and could cause an embolism, an obstruction in a vessel that could kill her, if she lay there without getting up, especially if she started to hyperventilate.

One morning when I was at school and my mother was home alone with her, Nana started to hyperventilate.

Stop that, my mother said.

Hhhheup-hoo, was the sound Nana made, *hhhheup-hoo*.

You're doing that on purpose, squeaked my mother. *Stop it!* But Nana would not stop. A note was delivered to me in class, asking me to come see the dean, and that was how I heard.

YOU THINK YOU *should* be sad. You are *expected* to be sad, you feel guilty about not being sad. In which case you feel *something*— guilt, which is not a reaction to the death directly but a reaction to having no reaction.

You recriminate yourself. In some ways these recriminations are the worst of all, worse even than when you feel glad about a death. Feeling nothing at all when someone dies whom you believed you loved suggests psychosis. Or, worse, inhumanity—you are a stone, say, or a mollusk. A robot, a stick figure, a wire.

Feeling nothing about a death is often even harder to admit to yourself, and reveal to others, than feeling glad. Others will think you are lying. They will believe you are in denial. They will tell you to have a good cry.

If you fail to cry, they will worry. A set of mind games will ensue. Playing these games—you want to feel, you want to please—you will hear yourself lying, feigning, faking it. This will make you hate and fear yourself even more. In horror you will watch yourself crying crocodile tears. When you are done, you will hardly know your own name.

NANA'S FUNERAL WAS a few days before my birthday. This made me feel ripped off, because that date was now going to be an annual day of family mourning. My father cried at the funeral. It was the first and only time I ever saw him cry. He laid his face in his hands and started to shake. And all those years before, he had never even seemed to like Nana much. Her white coffin topped with a white bouquet looked small, almost like luggage. I remember nothing else. My mind wandered to what was going on outside the chapel and to what people were wearing.

My birthday quietly came and went. My mother was in deep mourning. She spent the days in housecoats, racked with sobs. I skulked around, wanting to feel but unable to. One day I embraced my mother—held out my arms to her and said, *It's awful, isn't it?*

It is, she sobbed. *It is!* She clung to me, convulsing, as I told myself to act the way she acted—then I would feel as she felt. But

I could not. I stood there like an obelisk, watching my face in the mirror behind her back, freckled and sun-burnished and blank.

I was not incapable of emotion. A few months before, a boy I liked said he was sick of me and I cried pails. Now my own flesh and blood was gone forever and I felt nothing, and why? Because I was a thoughtless brat? Because I was sixteen? My *mother's mother*, I kept saying to myself. *Mom's mom*. It brought to mind a picture of concentric circles, of which I was one. Yet circles are abstract.

Nana did me no harm. Imagining her now, all these years later, I see an intelligent girl who as one of ten sisters and brothers could not afford college, a young woman coerced into marrying a nice yet incompatible stranger; I see a department-store manager—quite a good job for a woman in those days—whose whole life was about her career. Then I see her as a New Yorker transported in old age to bright, seasonless California. All these years later I see a life, I see seersucker shifts, I see a personality. And—looking at a box in my desk drawer of her monogrammed stationery, embossed cream on white—I feel something. A twinge. A pang. But it is her life that hurts rather than her death, and it hurts me now rather than then.

She never did me harm, but I never had *fun* with her—though one time we were in a steakhouse with a make-your-own sundae buffet and, instead of ordering ice cream, Nana went up with an empty coffee cup and filled it with toppings. *As good as a sundae—ice cream just wastes space!* she said, but to the adults at the table, not to me; nor did she engage me as she sat there eating the mingled toppings with a spoon. That was it: she did not engage me. With my mother she was thoroughly engaged. And my mother was thoroughly engaged with her. I was extraneous.

Jeannette and I were playing catch in the park two weeks after Nana died. Jeannette shouted across the grass, *How do you feel?*

Feel about what? I said, fumbling the ball.

I WAS SO young. Not an infant but fifteen and then sixteen, and a very infantile sixteen. Marcel Proust was scarcely older than that when *his* grandmother died. He watched his mother go into deep mourning for her mother, trudging on a beach in the rain so that her wetness would illustrate her distress. Yet as far as he could tell, Proust himself felt nothing—until two years later, when, bending over to tie his shoelaces one day, he was suddenly overwhelmed with sorrow, then with guilt for its having taken so long to surface. Marguerite Duras was only seven when her father died. As an adult, famous for the passion she conveyed in such novels as *The Lover*, she would boast about the death's lack of effect on her: "I obviously felt no emotion. No sadness, no tears, no questions." Duras mused, "He was away on a trip when he died. A few years later I lost my dog. I was inconsolable. Never had I suffered so much."

Grief is largely lost on the young. They cry over disasters that affect them tangibly. They understand that much. At subtler types of loss, the young blink uncomprehendingly. To the young, just about anyone older is old enough to die. The young are shielded from the worst horror because they cannot fathom it. They are oblivious, which is refreshing and appalling. *Youth holds no society with grief,* wrote Euripides.

My friend Craig lost both of his parents within a month: his mother to a sudden illness and his father to a massive coronary which required no imagination to interpret as a broken heart. During that month and in the days after, Craig and his wife would come home from the hospital and from work, slump on their sofa, and watch their toddler daughter play happily on the floor. To her those days were no worse than any others—a bit better, in fact, because her aunts, uncles, and cousins were around more than usual. On the night Craig became an orphan, he watched his child march in circles around the living room, wearing a dress-up bowler hat, beating a toy drum, and chanting *Happy! Happy! Happy!* at the top of her lungs. Craig felt sick, then felt blessed. In the midst of misery a little girl felt no pain, and neither did the flowers in the yard outside, and neither did the sky.

The very young have been known to cry more over the deaths of pets than those of grandparents, and to cry more over a canceled trip to Disneyland than a global epidemic. The very young make no apologies in this regard. Teenagers know enough to know, when they feel nothing, that this is not how they are *supposed* to feel. Teenagers know enough to lie.

But it is not only the young who feel nothing.

My ex-boyfriend Reed had an ordinary family life until he was seven years old, when his father moved out and took up with a new girlfriend. Thenceforth, Reed saw his father only sporadically: every few weeks, sometimes every few months.

Restless in the house where his clinically depressed mother lay alternately crying in bed and threatening to kill his father, Reed began spending more and more time at the lively home of his best friend, Martin Welsh. He went home with Martin every day after school, then stayed for dinner—lovingly prepared by Martin's mother, served by Martin's two sisters, and presided over by Martin's father, Bert. A connoisseur in many fields, Bert had been a foreign correspondent in China during the revolution and in India and Egypt and Russia and spoke seven languages and always had something interesting to say. Reed was sure Bert was a secret agent or a communist or something similarly exotic. At the dinner table and on outings—Reed was always invited along—Bert led the kids, the boys especially, in word games and tongue twisters (in seven languages) and guessing games entailing characters and anecdotes from his many adventures abroad. *Guess who was inside the tent with the pasha? Guess!* Reed usually had the fastest and funniest answers, which often had Bert in stitches.

Nearly every weekend, Reed slept over. He celebrated Christmas and his birthday with the Welshes, only dimly aware of the pity they all felt for him as they gave him presents to open—his mother couldn't be bothered with holidays, and his father rarely sent a gift. By the time he and Martin started high school, Reed had spent so much time at the Welsh house that its interiors— its Chinese watercolors and Persian rugs—were as familiar as those of his own home, and inhabited his dreams just as much. The books Bert had given him to read—atlases of the Indian subcontinent, picture books with French text—were the ones he would remember all his life.

Reed and Martin drifted apart at age thirteen, as child-hood friends do, when one of them started dating girls and the other did not. Reed no longer went home with Martin every day. Those days when he did, it was always awkward, because there were always other guys around—new friends—and usually a girl. Reed still spent Christmas with the Welshes: Bert holding court, even as the neurological disease that was consuming him slowed the jokes on his lips and sent his drinks sloshing over the rims of monogrammed tumblers and onto the rug.

Reed was traveling in Europe the summer after finishing college when he received a letter saying that Bert was dead. The neurological disease had weakened him; then bone cancer in his leg finished him off. That leg—which in neatly pressed trousers had bounced jauntily under the family table every night. That leg—which had climbed the Great Wall, raised dust clouds in the Gobi Desert and plied the Silk Road. That leg—Reed sat on the steps of a cathedral and realized that, beyond the cartoon-ish images in his head of the leg doing this and that, juxtaposed with science-textbookish diagrams of its afflicted bone, he felt nothing at all. The sun played across his forehead as he contem-plated this. He folded the letter and slipped it into his backpack and got up to go.

It was not *good* news about Bert, *obviously*. It was *bad* news, ostensibly, but Reed did not feel bad about it. Walking along the crowded street, he tried to feel bad for a minute or two, the way you might try on a shoe. But it would not stay; the bad feeling kept sliding away.

This can't be right, Reed scolded himself. He stopped, removing the letter from his pack, unfolding it and reading it again. It was from his mother. *Bert went into a hospice at the very end.* The word *hospice* gave Reed a chill, but not the news itself. The news itself seemed very distant, and nothing to do with him.

Bert was part of his past. Thinking of him now, Reed felt no regrets, no pang for anything he might have done or should have done, no anger, no resentment. And no love. He pictured the Welsh siblings and their mother standing, holding hands, around a bed in which the dead Bert lay. He saw it as if through a periscope. He saw how sad they were. But had not Bert enjoyed more adventure in one lifetime than three average men in their average lives combined? And was not Bert, at eighty, old enough to go in peace?

But he was like a father to me!

Like a father. In the absence of his own. Bert was the one who passed the peas to Reed across the table and asked how his day had been. Bert was the one who bought Reed gifts. *And this is all the thanks he gets?* Reed shivered. Because yes, it was.

It struck him then that death is a truth serum. When we are together and alive, we walk and talk and laugh and seem to love, but also, without even knowing it, we lie. We go along with it. For the sake of convenience or appearances or custom or because he or she is just there. And we think, *Yes he is my friend, of course she is my grandmother, of course he is my surrogate father.* We do not, together and alive, interrogate each other or ourselves about the exact quantity of our affection. Then they die and, looking back, we realize with a start what it all meant, and wonder did we *ever* care. We realize then how vast and fragile was that artifice, and wonder who else in our lives could leave us now, right now, and whose dying—to our surprise—would stir us no more than a spring breeze stirs a stone. And that would be the worst part of it as the days pass, our surprise.

ANOTHER KIND OF apathy comes later. Say you felt sorrow at first. Say you were wracked with it. Then a day comes when you feel a little less wracked. Time heals. That is the best news in the world and also the worst. "I missed the attacks of grief," John Bayley noted a few years after the death of his wife, the novelist Iris Murdoch, "which came on with the suddenness of asthma or a toothache. The difference being that each bout had an indescribable and physical happiness about it. More like sex in a way than misery." With regret, he mourned the loss of mourning. When it starts to ebb, you ask yourself, What kind of monster must I be to have forgotten for an hour, a day, a week? To sit here swinging my feet, eating this hamburger and having this conversation as if—

As if.

My friend Harper was with his son at 7-Eleven to buy Slurpees when he noticed a familiar face behind him in the checkout line. A name surfaced to go with the face. Harper exchanged hand slaps with his old high school friend and former tennis partner Rico, who had come to the store with *his* little boy to buy Cokes. The two kids eyed each other shyly as Rico and Harper brought each other up to date on their doings over the past twelve years—wives, kids, houses, jobs. Rico told Harper that he was in the lumber industry. After the men made their purchases, they sauntered outside, exchanged phone numbers, and parted with hearty waves. Harper never got around to calling Rico, nor did he hear from his old pal. He kept telling himself to dig out Rico's number and arrange a get-together, but his wife was pregnant again and things, as he puts it now, just kept getting in the way.

Then one day his wife handed him the morning paper. She raised her eyebrows: *Is this that guy you said you saw?*

Under a photograph of a smiling Rico was the headline *Southside Man Killed.* A load of logs had not been fastened properly onto a truck bed and as Rico stood on the shoulder of the road trying to fix the problem they slid off, crushing him.

Harper felt himself go white. He thought of Rico's timid son and the redheaded wife Rico had told him about. Remorse for never having called his old friend flooded through Harper. And so did something else: a jarring certainty that he had run into Rico at 7-Eleven that day for a reason. It wasn't a mere fluke—Harper was sure he was meant to learn a lesson from this sequence of events, and the lesson was this: Cherish what you have. All is fleeting. Don't let opportunities slip by.

He vowed then and there to absorb this lesson, and then he announced it to his wife. He rushed into the TV room to hug his startled little boy.

And for the next few weeks, what he had learned from the Rico incident stayed *so* clear in his head. Every day seemed so precious. Every mishap at the office seemed absurd compared with the sheer joy of being alive. Every meal with his family, every ride in his car, every chat with a friend made Harper shiver at the magnitude of his luck. He devised little rituals of gratitude—silent salutes, rhymes to remember—to practice throughout the day.

And then he stopped.

Not all at once, but bit by bit. One less rhyme on the drive home, when the traffic was backed up for miles. When his son broke the remote control, one less hug.

It was barely a month after reading about Rico's death that Harper realized with a start that he hadn't felt grateful or joyful or lucky all day. He hadn't thought of Rico at all. Harper went to his wife looking crestfallen.

I can't believe it, he kept saying, punching himself in the temple with his fist. *It's like his death had no meaning at all.*

She consoled him. She said it doesn't dishonor the dead to let them slip our minds sometimes. She said it isn't possible to keep them in the forefront all the time, even those we loved best. Even when we want to sustain that level of intensity, she said softly, we can't.

Life goes on, Harper's wife said. That was the best news. Also the worst.

7.

disgust

IT WAS GETTING to the point where every time I checked
my e-mail and found one from Veronica, a jolt ran
through me. Sex, danger, anger, sadness, and a wild wordless
feeling, a vicarious racing-down-the-street-in-red-lipstick-long-
earrings-miniskirt-and-tube-top-that-says-CUTE! kind of rush,
a mad panic halfway between horror and thrill. All of this
arrived packed into that one name, not her actual name but
the handle she used for e-mails, Siamesecat8, and it was all
because Veronica was having an affair with a married man.
Well, separated, so his marriage did not count. At least, not to
Veronica. One morning, she wrote:

*Terrible news!!! Corey told me last night that he doesn't want to see
me anymore. He met someone else—the woman of his dreams, he
says—and he asked her out! I told him that what he was saying was
killing me. He laughed. He actually laughed!!! He said he thought
he could get it up three times in one night for her.*

Why does it hurt so much? Maybe because now I see I meant

nothing to him—just a coffee break before starting something really good. He sounded so happy, that jerk. Can you believe he still owes me $1,600?

Look, don't be shocked but I decided to kill myself. I looked up on the Internet how to do it and I have all the ingredients, and it won't hurt, I promise. You know what a chicken I am—I wouldn't do anything that hurt even a little bit!

Please remember that you're my friend and don't worry.

I was hardly finished reading it when she called.

Look, said Veronica. She had long since given up on preambles, introductions, hello. *I was going to do it this morning but I didn't have time.*

Ah, this speedy text-messaging age of ours. No time to kill herself!

What did you buy? I said. *What do you mean: ingredients?*

While saying this, I realized that there is no proper tone in which to ask such a question, no etiquette, a total absence of those preordained social protocols that the Japanese call *kata.* We were talking about death but we were not. We were talking about shopping but we were not. Since I was twelve I have chatted with girlfriends about trips to the mall, to Melrose Avenue, to thrift stores: *What'd you score? A blue one? Coo-wull!* But now: this morning the words started pretty much the same, but weren't. I realized I was furious, I was out of patience, because this was not the first time she had said this sort of thing, but I was terrified, and I was also curious. That part of me, that relentless distant part clicking away like a surveillance camera, yearned to know what Veronica had bought. Not so that I could call the cops and order them to drive to her apartment and find it, though I knew I should, but just because I wanted to know. What was it, how did she dress for the shopping trip, did she carry a list? I thought she had. She was the organized type of person who would. Did the clerk fling Veronica's purchases heedlessly into a bag after ringing them up, the way they do at Walgreen's, or did he wrap them up stoutly, wrist sinews thick, the way they do at hardware stores? That would depend, of course, on what she'd bought.

I'm not going to tell you, said Veronica in a voice as neat and pert as a cookie cutter piercing dough. She clearly knew she was going to say this, long before I asked. *I'm not going to tell you because you'll just come over here and find it and take it away.*

Come on, I whined. *What'd you buy?*

Nope. It's a secret, said Veronica. Cross-legged on my bed, watching birds hop from branch to branch outside, I realized she was being playful. *It's a seeecret*, like a toddler who has hidden your car keys. The power. The puzzle. She had not sounded so merry in years.

In which case—nor had she sounded quite so alive. Even at Christmas the previous winter, her favorite time of year, her voice had been its usual teeth-clenched drone, low and slow if Corey had canceled an assignation, high and bright if the date was still on, if he hadn't canceled it yet. Did I mention that Corey is an alcoholic with a DUI on his record, a gambling problem and a shopping addiction and major debts, and looks like a movie star?

Now she sounded like a party guest.

I was going to do it this morning but I didn't have time. The method takes eight hours to work and the landlord said he was sending someone over here at noon to fix the radiator.

Eight hours?

I was thinking: Couldn't be wrist-slitting then. Couldn't be hanging. Shooting. Jumping off a building. Those only take minutes. Ticking options off a list—I tried to stop but the list kept getting longer, with a corresponding filmstrip in my head, Veronica leaping, Veronica with gun muzzle between lips, Veronica seizing a razor, Veronica submerged in a bathtub full of warm water slowly turning pink with blood. Stop. Stop. She was doing this to me. She was making me do this.

Why does it take a whole eight hours?

I said I'm not going to tell you.

I just asked a simple question, I said, sounding like my mother.

I said it's a secret. It just takes eight hours, OK?

But wouldn't it just be—

I almost said: *Wouldn't it just be faster to shoot yourself?*

I have always given Veronica advice, because she has always asked for it: What color should she dye her hair? Who sells the cutest nail decals? How can she go anywhere now that her car has been totaled? She always asked, with varying degrees of desperation, and I always came up with something, because that's what really helps those who come to you in need, isn't it? More than hugging and sighing and saying, *There there.* At which I am really bad anyway. A pragmatic answer, instructions, something concrete to do. Because they ask. Why else would they ask? Ash blonde. NailZone. Ride the bus. And now: *Wouldn't it just be faster to—*

Not that she always did what I said, anyway. She detested buses, for example.

But if Veronica did not ask me how to commit suicide, and looked up the instructions online, then that meant she took advice from someone else, not me. Some helpful stranger on the Internet. Something was rising in my throat. It was envy.

I swallowed it away, that perverse tang.

But it was relief, too, because if she had looked up the instructions online, no one, after she was gone, could point a finger at me and say: it was YOU who told Veronica how.

I was supposed to feel only sorrow and panic and the desire to save her life.

Look, if anybody found me sooner than eight hours, Veronica was saying, *then I could be rescued. That's what I don't want.* The filmstrip sped up in my head. You hear about how corpses look: poignantly lifelike, as if sleeping, if you find them soon enough; or, if not, bellies so swollen with gas that you could burst them with a pin, jaws slack or blown completely off. The film ripped and flapped, nattering.

It's painless, said Veronica. *Don't worry.*

What a stupid thing to say.

But it's OK. That was so like Veronica. Delivering awful news with a smile.

It's fine.

It isn't fine, I burst out, in a voice like broken crackers. You're not fooling me with your false cheer. *I wanna keeell myself,* I said, mocking her accent, *but eeet's fine.*

I'm serious, she said. *See, I'll be happier.*

How do you know you will? You won't be anything. It's nothingness.

That sounds better than this.

Better than what?

Better than Corey sleeping with someone else.

So let me get this straight: in the whole world of possibilities, your only alternatives are sleeping with Corey or eternal nothingness?

Death, she said in a dreamy voice, *would be a—a different place.* Veronica had always yearned to travel. *Death,* she said now, brightly, *will be an adventure.*

But what if it's not? I sounded shrill. *What if it's just boring but then it's too late to turn back?*

She didn't say anything for a while. That was her new style. None of that old *Hmm, wow, how interesting, you really think so?* which made her appear to be a good listener. This was her new style, where she took a long time to answer or never did at all, not looking at you, because her mind was somewhere else. Sometimes, such as right then, you could practically hear her drumming her nails. This was her new style, where she need not boost your ego anymore or pretend anything or evince anything save that she was miserable and yearned to die. Her new style, a suicide style.

HER THERAPIST PUT her on suicide watch. For a whole week Veronica had to call the therapist every two hours to prove she was alive. This was the most interesting thing that had happened to me in months, and it wasn't even really happening to me. And yet it was. But it was not. I shouldn't talk about it with others. I shouldn't be telling you, certainly. Hearing me talk about it, you think I don't care. You think I mock Veronica, that I am toying with her abject misery, but I am not. I just don't know what else to do with it, with what she said, with why, with what Veronica wanted to do.

All her e-mails that week were short and described various aspects of unhappiness. They all ended with the same sentence, which was not really a sentence but a prepositional phrase: on suicide watch.

Then on Sunday, she called. Her voice was high and bubbly and I was glad at first but by then I really should have known.

Corey called! she said.

She sounded like a happy lady in a black-and-white comedy film who fusses and giggles as she tries on diamond rings or frosts a cake.

He might not go out with his dream girl again. Veronica was breathless. *They got into a huge fight about his drinking. Ha ha! Anyway he's on his way over here now.*

But what if he makes up with her and you're just—

I can't wait to see him! said Veronica. *Which color thong d'you think I should wear?*

But, I said, sounding now like Mrs. Warren, my seventh-grade sex-ed teacher, *if you, um, make yourself too available to him—*

She was impatient. *I have to go now.*

Look, I said, *the world is full of nice guys.*

A sigh came down the line, a muffled *tiktiktik*. Her nails.

SUICIDE IS SO selfish. But we must not speak ill of the dead.

We might get angry at the dead. Angry at fate. Angry at life. We are told this is natural, a passing phase. We might get angry at medicine or God—to the point of suing a hospital, or turning our backs and walking away, faith and belief sluicing out of us like wine from a cracked jug, hands clamped over our ears so as not to hear any lordly entreaties, just in case.

We are told this is normal. But we must not speak ill of the dead, per se, not actually blame them or anything because they did not mean to leave us.

But what if they did?

Suicides punish those who are left behind. When Hunter S. Thompson killed himself in 2005, he was in the middle of a telephone conversation with his wife. Without a word of warning, the iconoclastic journalist blew off his head. She heard the bang, then silence. Thompson shot himself in the kitchen—while his son, daughter-in-law, and six-year-old grandson were in nearby rooms just a few yards away. Are we to applaud this as yet another daring, outrageous feat?

In elementary school I knew a pair of twins: always together, laughing, playing hopscotch just the two of them in matching jumpers and striped shirts like some trick of the camera, four look-alike long legs in white tights. Teachers would ask, *Can your parents tell you apart?* and they would chorus, *No, but our big brother can!* Their brother who called them Eeny and Meeny and loaned them his hippie hats to wear at Halloween. One day in sixth grade the twins did not come to school. Our young teacher, who wore white frosted lipstick, sat smoothing her skirt and told us Eeny and Meeny had come home after school the day before to find their brother in the basement hanging by his neck. They changed schools after that, or moved away, or stopped going to school. I never saw the twins again.

My mother fumed when I told her about the brother. *He was old enough to know who would discover him!* My mother always fumes at those who kill themselves. Last year her friend Eva was engaged to a man who slit his wrists on their brand-new king-size bed, leaving no note. Eva was downstairs at the time, consulting with the caterer. *Why get engaged at all?* my mother raged. *Why buy Eva a ring? Was that a joke?* Imagine Eva having to get out her guest list now, my mother said, and having to call everyone and say the wedding was canceled and tell them why.

My mother fumes at those who kill themselves because she knows. Sometimes she calls them brutal and sometimes she calls them cowards but this is partly because she envies them. After my father had his stroke, she looked at me and said, *I wanted to die first!* She said she had been hoping to find a lump in her breast but tell no one until it was too late. *Then he could be a widower and just have fun.* No lump. No luck. A month later at the cemetery, she warned me not to be "surprised" at what she might do now. She signaled quotation marks with her fingers. We were in the thick tussocky grass high up the slope between where my father lay in his niche and my grandparents lay in theirs. Below us spread the haze of Los Angeles in mid-afternoon, a stippled glint. And I thought: Look at all those people down there, in their cars and offices and swimming pools, in parking lots and on patios. They have the will to live. Such a simple thing, and yet I have a dead father who never wanted to die and dead grandparents who were *comme ci comme ça* about life and now a living mother who wants to die, who is standing here "warning" me about what she "might" "have" to "do."

I felt sorry for her but, squinting at those graves and the city, I also felt mean.

Sure, I said. *Whatever.*

She made her voice gravelly and stern: *This doesn't mean I don't love you.*

OK.

She wanted something. What? A shouted *Noooooo,* a plea? *I beg you—don't!* Yet I was not going to give her that. Like the girl on the beach I used to be, the dazed imperturbable girl, I stared at her without expression, as if staring into sand. I shrugged.

I might, she hissed.

OK. Bluffer, I thought.

She did not, and I have to hand it to her that she did not, because life became bad without him, and she got sick—not with something that kills, but things that hurt and make you look ridiculous. She broke one leg and learned to walk again, then broke the other leg. In bed the second time, she started in again with *I don't want to live, why should I live.*

I looked out the window. *Don't make me have this conversation.*

She asked, in a light tone, pretending to just be curious, by what method my friend Jeff's mother killed herself. *Oh by the way, remember your friend Jeff? I was just wondering—did you mention something about tape and a plastic bag?*

I shut the curtain. *Stop it.*

I asked you a simple question.

Walking back to the house from the hospital those nights, I would stare from the sidewalk into the lights of oncoming cars. I had to steel myself, picture my husband, to keep from leaping in front of them. I do not know why I wanted to run headlong into traffic, now, exactly. I think a mother's desire to die might be contagious for an only child.

She did not do it, then, or since, which is quite something.

But she knows. She knows how it feels not to want to get up. Not to bother, and not to have to keep making up reasons why. When she calls Eva's fiancé *a sadist bastard*, my mother is not engaging in mere moralistic prattle. She thinks of Eva waiting on line at the returns counter with her wedding dress while wondering what she did wrong.

FOR WHATEVER REASONS, a suicidal person can't expunge his or her misery while still alive. Can't walk out of it. Can't quench it. Can't wrestle it into something else, some constructive activity such as marathon running or empathy or art, that saves them. Can't get far enough away for perspective. Feeling trapped in a burning house, the suicidal person can't articulate this sensation expertly enough for friends, family, and therapists to see its gravity, swoop in and stage a rescue.

Save me. That's what some suicides say.

Others say: *Leave me alone. This has nothing to do with you, but— gotta go.*

And those who mourn, who walk not on eggshells but barefoot over shattered crystal ever after, wondering, *Was it my fault? Will it happen again?* remember all the talk that cycled nowhere, all the kindnesses and sympathies and the attempts to cheer. They remember the balms given that appeared, at the time, to work. All failed.

And this might make a mourner not just sad but mad.

Fast or slow, self-destruction destroys more than just a self, and we the living get stuck with the bills.

WESTERN RELIGIONS REVILE suicide as a great sin. The corpses of suicides are traditionally banned from burial in hallowed ground. Christianity holds that human life is God's property, so to destroy a life is to steal from God and attempt to usurp His power. Similarly, Judaism considers suicide another form of murder, and argues that one's own soul is not one's to extinguish. And a prevailing theme in secular Western thought is that suicide is an insult to humanity itself. In his influential essay *On Liberty*, the nineteenth-century philosopher John Stuart Mill argued that since the crux of liberty is the individual's power to make choices, then any choice that precludes that individual from being able to make further choices should be prevented.

AS IT HAPPENED, Veronica did not kill herself. After her week on suicide watch, she stabilized, according to her therapist, and one day we had coffee. She was trying to explain in a flat, laundry-list tone why Corey was worth dying over. *He just is.* I kept asking myself why I felt sick. Was it because she was my friend, because I loved her? Was it because I saw so clearly (or so I thought) her potential and what we stood to lose? She sighed as she spoke, making it all sound so negligible, so transitory, so slippery, so arguable, her hold on the world. So optional, so arbitrary, so ambivalent, so feeble: still up for debate, still undecided really, as if to say, Give me time and I'll get back to you on that. She sounded impatient as she spoke, an impression fueled by the noise she was making, her long painted nails drumming the tabletop, *tiktik*.

She did not kill herself then, but the things she said, the way she said them, made it very clear that she certainly could. She *could*. It all depended—on Corey, or guys like Corey.

THOSE WHO HAVE fought in vain to live: another week, another month—what would those millions have given for just that much? To walk and talk for just that long, to love one minute more? All those who, down the ages, begged for a reprieve but received none: talking to Veronica, I thought about them and became furious. *You ingrate*, I seethed at her silently. *You idiot, you thief.* All those on sickbeds and battlefields this very minute—*Veronica*, I thought, *they would trade you.* They would pay you anything just to be you. As would those men I have seen in Mexico who, lacking the lower halves of their bodies, propel their top halves around on double-wide skateboards. And the beggar-lady I once saw in Lisbon who had no eyes: not even slits, or scars, or hollows where eyes should have been—just a smooth surface like that of an apple. Standing in that doorway murmuring to passersby, she too would pay you to switch. As Albert Camus once wrote to a friend: "Such is man, through the centuries, proud to live a single instant." Veronica is pretty, she is healthy, her family is rich. And yet she ached to die while elsewhere in the world even slaves strive to live. The sun, the rain, cheeseburgers—Veronica would just throw it away. She just wanted peace and quiet and a kind of adventure but her very appetite for death was a form of disrespecting the dead.

Micheline Maurel, a survivor of the Ravensbrück concentration camp, wrote after her ordeal: "Be happy, you who live in fine apartments, in ugly houses or in hovels. Be happy, you who have your loved ones, and you also who sit alone and dream and can weep. Be happy, you who torture yourselves over metaphysical problems, and you who suffer because of money worries. Be happy, you the sick who are being cared for, and you who care for them, and be happy, oh how happy, you who die a death as normal as life, in hospital beds or in your homes. Be happy, all of you: millions of people envy you."

SUICIDE IS THE sword of Damocles, swinging over those whom the dead one leaves behind, swoosh. A suicide in the family is one of those grim legacies, like madness or hereditary illness, about which in good conscience intended marriage partners should be told. It is a matter of disclosure. *Look, I've got something to tell you.* Suicides are also major family secrets, literal skeletons in closets. The grandfather of one of my best childhood friends shot and killed himself five years before her birth—right in our town. We all knew her sprightly grandmother, and knew she was a widow, but not why. Not that it was our business, you might say. But all those countless times in grade school, and then through high school and college, when anyone else mentioned grandfathers—*Mine gave me a car! Mine's senile!*—this friend said nothing at all. Her grandfather was simply "dead." Not until she became a mother herself did I learn the truth, and not because she told me. All those years she had been too ashamed or disgusted to tell us, or her parents were ashamed and swore her to a secrecy which at first might have puzzled a small girl but in time became set in stone. As if descendants of a suicide still bear the mark. Or as if they might pick up guns and shoot themselves, anytime, *right now.*

My friend Jeff and his sister Amber were in college when their mother killed herself by taking sedatives before sealing her head inside a plastic bag. It was not her first suicide attempt, nor her first choice of method, but this was the one that worked. Jeff is a lawyer and Amber is a doctor now. They loved their mother and still do. Yet they go rigid when they speak of her. Amber laughs bitterly and says: *Suicide is the ultimate "Fuck you."*

VERONICA CAME RIGHT out and announced her intentions. She was just as frankly deliberate as the suicide whose corpse Langston Hughes once saw in Mexico: "I noticed a small crowd of Indians in their serapes, standing around the shallow basin of the fountain in the center of the park," he later wrote. "I looked down and there, in scarcely three feet of water, lay the body of a young woman, curled about the base of the fountain. She was nicely dressed, and obviously of a decent family. The police found a suicide note . . . *what* will power it must have taken to drown oneself in a shallow fountain hardly as deep as your knees!" That kind of determination is maddening, yet there is another kind of self-destruction—slow but sure. Addicts, alcoholics, chain-smokers, engagers in unsafe sex, diabetics and asthmatics and those with weak hearts who are casually careless about their medications: they know what they are doing. Some pretend not to know. *What? I feel fine.* Some lie. *I gave that stuff up years ago!* Some are deliberate. *Don't try to stop me, man.*

Loved ones beg them to stop. Doctors and cops warn them to stop. *You're killing yourself, can't you see?* They can. They can't. My friend Kit used to share a house with two young men who died a few days apart. One was a speed addict who shot himself, apparently on impulse, at the end of a three-day tweak. The other was a heroin addict who overdosed—although Kit says he had been self-destructing for a long time in more ways than one:

He would say something obnoxious to you just to see you react. He knew exactly what to say that would drive you crazy, and he'd say it. He wanted to provoke everyone. He picked fights with everyone. It's as if he was hoping to get beaten up or stabbed. That guy was on a freight train headed straight to death. I think he was trying to get someone to kill him because he was just afraid to do it himself.

ONE DAY IN a nice neighborhood I saw two workmen hauling items out of a house and throwing them into a Dumpster. Lamps, potted cactus plants, stereo equipment, suits—it all looked so new. A woman was supervising the workmen from the porch. Seeing me stop to look, she shrugged.

You want it? Take it. She rubbed her arms, even though the day was hot. *I mean it. Whatever you want.*

The men were upending desk drawers into the Dumpster. Papers tumbled out, stacks of carefully bound files, and from one drawer a shiny stream of money.

Go on, said the woman. *I don't care.*

One of the men walked out of the garage swinging a ship-in-a-bottle in each hand.

I took those. And the money and the suits.

The woman told me in a beaten drone that her husband had died the previous week of a heart attack. *Sitting at that damn desk!* For years he had been warned. For years.

You smell that shit? She waved her arms. It was true. The Dumpster and the whole yard reeked of cigarette smoke.

I asked her if she was throwing away anything she might regret. I said a friend of mine who lost her son gave his fossil collection to a thrift shop and regretted it.

Fuck it!

The men were hefting a corduroy beanbag chair into the Dumpster and stomping it down to make it fit.

Fuck it, she said. *Fuck it all.*

8.

foreboding

A MOMENT COMES when you first realize your life will
end, someday: that everyone else's will, too—that life
is a series of endings that come crashing down like steel gates
one after the other, and there's nothing you can do but look
back, and ahead, and back, and wonder, and wait.

A 1930s black-and-white romantic comedy was on TV, all
jaunty soundtrack and feminine twitters as my mother started
preparing dinner and I erected something with Tinkertoys on
the carpet next to the window in the day's last brothy sunlight.
The film was as alien to me as if it were foreign, with its fops
in cravats and wide lapels and ladies in fox furs, addressing
servants in affected accents—*Maisie, who delivahed this styoopid
lettuh?*

Mom nodded as an actor strode down a grand curving staircase. *Dead,* she said, gesturing toward him with a paring knife.
He died.

An actress in a pale gown, pale hair set in waves, ran after
him pleading for forgiveness.

Oh, her. Mom waved a potato ricer. *Dead.*

The camera traveled outdoors to a garden party where couples danced to a jazz combo under festoons of paper lanterns.

Dead. Mom pointed at each performer in turn as if she were shooting them down herself. *He's dead. She's dead.* She pointed at the couples dancing, and at the partygoers sipping cocktails at the pretty little tables. *Car accident. Parkinson's. That one,* she said, shaking her head, pointing at a brunette. *She got real fat when she got older, after she stopped acting in movies and bought a chain of pancake restaurants. She got so fat she had a heart attack.*

But, I said, *where are they all now?*

Mom shrugged. *I told you. Dead.*

But where?

Who knows? She flicked potato gratings back into the bowl. *Buried in graveyards.*

Before that day, I had heard the words *dead* and *die* countless times. I was five and the word came up in fairytales and songs. *I don't know why she swallowed that fly! Perhaps she'll die.* My parents knew people who had "died" and they talked to each other about it over my head, in the presumptive way of adults who think that if they use a certain effervescent tone of voice you will never suspect that they are discussing anything dire. But it was right *then* when the meaning suddenly came clear. You dance, you drink, you stride down curving staircases, and then one day you don't.

You *don't.* You can't.

You die. Why had I never fixed on these two words before as anything to ask about, to ponder? Because clearly death was momentous, and amounted to a really big problem. Somehow, bodies broke—life broke—and no one fixed them.

My father fixed things. He was an engineer, he could fix anything around the house—lamps and the sliding door and bamboo blinds. At work he fixed something called satellites. When he sat down with something to fix, he perspired—it was usually hot in Los Angeles—and his scalp reddened and he swore, always the same incantation, *goddamnsonofabitchbastard*. He squinted through his glasses at the broken thing, then in a flash he would see what was wrong with it and what to do.

Ya hafta find the glitch, he said.

Since bodies were so pervasive and so necessary, it made no sense that they broke but were not fixed. I was the smartest girl in the whole kindergarten class. I thought, *Ya hafta find the glitch*. I was the smartest girl.

In our backyard I found the dried corpse of a lizard missing one foot. Such corpses turned up a lot because the native species had no past experience with cats, which liked to stalk and kill them as they lazed on hot rocks thinking they had no natural predators. But the lizards must not have been tasty, because after a few nibbles the cats usually abandoned their prey, which quickly desiccated to the consistency of sticks. I put the small corpse in a glass of water on my dresser. One day later it was soft and supple, looking alive. Its eyes, which had been caved in, plumped out. *This* was the answer then. It hit me with a rush. I was a genius. We simply soak the dead.

The problem was . . .

The lizard would not move.

It would not move. I spoke to it.

The problem was . . .

I TRIED THE same thing with a sand crab and it didn't work. I tried it with a cricket and it didn't work. I tried it with snails. Nothing worked.

I prayed over the corpses. Nothing. Just the spreading silence of my yellow bedroom in the filtered light of my choo-choo-train lamp. My belief in resurrection fell away, resurrection by science or by God. We are helpless, I thought. And so began my fear, the morbid fear that gripped me then and has never let go. My fear of death is medieval in scope and style and infantility. Life in the modern world is far less reassuring than it should be to me, who sinks into superstition at the first sign of disorder and must steel myself and *force* myself to think of science. Like the Brotherhood of Flagellants—a sect whose adherents numbered well over 500,000 at its peak, who walked through fourteenth-century Europe whipping themselves believing that this could banish the Black Plague—I strive, as if it were possible, for control. Not that my forebodings are so extraordinary. Jean-Jacques Rousseau wrote that "he who pretends to look on death without fear lies . . . this is the great law of sentient beings, without which the entire human species would soon be destroyed."

When I was young I never wanted baby dolls. I shrank from the responsibility. I wanted no part of the gravity—now that I realized it was grave—of the fleshly necessities for which one rehearsed by playing with baby dolls. If I received such a doll as a gift, I cuddled it to be polite, then put it back into its box. It sat that way forever on a shelf, watching me balefully through its cellophane window with eyes (the box proclaimed) that could open and shut. Such dolls were manufactured to look helpless: bald, or with a furze of plastic hair, those eyes that flicked open as if entreating and clicked shut as if to say, *I'm sleeping. Now you must watch over me,* or, horrifyingly, *I'm dead.* Their bellies round and hard, their plastic limbs bent at the joints in a rictus of impotence and change-my-diapers-now and fear. Plastic is one thing, but flesh is another.

One day in first grade I went over to see my friend Wade after school. We were in his backyard making fruit-punch-flavored snow cones with his Mr. Frosty when his mother came into the yard holding his baby sister. I had barely ever seen a *real* baby, so I smiled—always polite—and backed away. *Would you like to hold her?* Mrs. Heller asked. *No thanks,* I said. *Are you afraid?* asked Mrs. Heller. *But holding babies is fun! Wade holds his baby sister all the time!* Wade blushed, digging his heel into the grass, nibbling a snow cone. *Come on,* Mrs. Heller coaxed. I made my arm go limp and flapped it. *Sorry!* I squeaked as if in surprise, as if I had just noticed it. *I can't! I have a broken arm!* How could I tell her then, how could I tell parents today, that the reason I do not want children is that they might die? Because we all do, but *they* die so *easily,* and I am cowardly, not brave.

Viewed from a certain angle I seem fearless. I have traveled. I do not fear bankruptcy, or dogs. I do not fear high places. I do not fear public speaking, though I do not like it—obviously. Who would? I do not fear strange foods. One day in Belgium, my husband and I were served blood sausage by our hosts. It was basically a large soft scab in a firm casing and because it was the local specialty, because we were being polite, we ate it. Just cut, chew and swallow, that's the way. I am not afraid of the ocean or the dark, even though the ocean hides sharks and riptides and the dark hides murderers. But these are abstract, these are anecdotes, compared to the black-and-whiteness, the *fact*, of death.

How could we be here, then just disappear without a trace?

Religions and philosophies and most grown-ups call ghosts by other names. They say *the soul*. They say *immortal soul*. Ghosts are unwelcome among Catholics, unless you count the Holy Ghost. We do not watch the comical adventures of Casper, the Friendly Soul. Yet the soul is a notoriously tricky concept to work out. No less a thinker than Aristotle himself lamented more than two thousand years ago that "to attain any assured knowledge about the soul is one of the most difficult things in the world." Wrestling with the concept for page after page, he concluded that the soul is pure essence, and that this essence makes itself manifest through the five senses, through thought and awareness. As for how this essence actually functions, again Aristotle struggles. "With what part of itself the soul discriminates sweet from hot I . . . must now describe again as follows: That with which it does so is a sort of unity, but in the way just mentioned, i.e., as a connecting term. And the two faculties it connects, being one by analogy and numerically, are each to each as the qualities discerned are to one another (for what difference does it make whether we raise the problem of discrimination between disparates or between contraries, e.g., white and black?). Let then C be to D as it is to B: it follows that C: A:: D: B. If then C and D belong to one subject, the case will be the same with them as with A and B. . . . The same reasoning holds if A be sweet and B white."

Aha. So there you go.

Sermons try to reassure us. Souls, the clergy say, go to *heaven* or *hell* or get lodged, like hairballs in plumbing, in between. I once visited the Museum of the Souls of the Dead in a church in Rome, where in wall-mounted glass display cases were night-gowns, hats, Bibles, and other articles bearing charred finger-prints said to have been made by souls trapped in purgatory attempting to attract the attention of their living relatives, whose prayers might help the stuck souls into heaven. Headstones offer up pathetic euphemisms that fool no one. *Sleep my darling. Mama's with the Lord.* But in real life, we burn with the same question I asked when I was five: *Where did the lizard go?*

Before Ralph Waldo Emerson became a famous essayist and poet, he was a Unitarian minister. But he struggled with con-ventional spirituality and his feelings about life and death. He became so obsessed with his own personal losses that he entered his family vault and pried open the caskets of his wife and son to ponder their contents. Fourteen months after the passing of his wife in 1832, Emerson noted in his journal: "I visited Ellen's tomb and opened her coffin." Sixteen years after the death of his five-year-old son Waldo, Emerson opened that coffin as well—desperately seeking, we can only surmise, perspective on the fragility of living and on how he might come to accept it.

Heaven and *hell* and *rest in peace* sound insubstantial, like a dodge.

I ache with wanting the dead to keep loving what they loved *then*, knowing what they knew. It is too much of a waste otherwise. Humanity frowns on waste. So, I imagine, would God. What—these personalities that took entire lifetimes to coalesce, and all they learned in their time: simply thrown away like non-recyclables? My father always said that when we die, we die, that nothing of us stays behind. *I'm a scientist*, he shrugged, hale and hearty at the time, digging in his garden. *That's what scientists believe.* But I cannot accept that he is gone, that all of them are gone. I cannot *stand* that somewhere, somehow, they do not still stroke the terrycloth that soothed them in their lives, still hating mayonnaise somewhere, somehow. Facing annihilation daily as a World War II pilot, Antoine de Saint-Exupéry, author of *The Little Prince*, confided in his journal: "I don't care if I'm killed in the war. But what will remain of what I have loved? ... not just people but customs, certain indispensable intonations, a certain spiritual radiance. What will remain of the farmhouse lunch under the olive trees of Provence, or of Handel?"

Does everything you ever were and ever knew vanish as your organs melt into sludge? I cannot stand that. I *cannot.*

I have a problem with the end of continuity as it pertains to life.

I LOVED THE Halloween carnival at school, where a classroom was transformed into a haunted house, with cobwebs made of fishnets and with agonized mumbles emerging from a tape deck: *Helllp meee.* Pressed into the orange frosting on cupcakes for sale in the sunshine were tiny plastic ghosts. I took ghosts so seriously. I hated Disneyland's Haunted Mansion because it *didn't* take ghosts seriously. I read ghost stories all the time. I read them instead of *Winnie the Pooh* and instead of *Charlie and the Chocolate Factory* and *Stuart Little* and *The Hobbit* and, later, instead of *Seventeen*. Ghost stories were in books and so they must be true. In their evanescent, ludicrous, talk-in-Scottish-accents way, ghosts seemed the only hope, the only proof, the only evidence of a life after death: the only ones with anything to say. I read ghost-story books that had been written for children and then turned to ghost stories written for adults. These favored subtitles such as "investigating the supernatural" and "journeys into the unexplained" and "modern frontiers of parapsychology." I lay awake at night shuddering, staring up at my bedroom ceiling as foghorns blared in the harbor, my mind running and rerunning images gleaned from ghost stories:

A bluff where a fairground used to be, above a beach: the spectral carousel spinning on wizened grass as merry-go-round music goes *plinkplonkplink* and long-dead children laugh and, far below, the crashing of the surf.

The wooden stairs in an old house, ascended by a disembodied pair of army boots, battered and scuffed and smeared with blood, accompanied by the chant: *Blooooody boots! Goin' up the first stair, blooooody boots! Goin' up the second stair.*

A haunted classroom in a boarded-up, abandoned school, where in the doorway stands the apparition of a boy, translucent, one hand cradling his swollen jaw as he whimpers in the desperate voice of the doomed, *It hurts.*

Steaming under a silver moon, a ship in whose wake bob

the ghostly heads of two sailors buried at sea. The captain says, *Full speed ahead*, but the two ghostly faces keep pace, gazing up from the white spume at their crewmates standing transfixed in the stern.

SINCE THE DAWN of civilization, humans have flirted with ghosts—with our genetic inability to reconcile ourselves to some incontrovertible *end*. Ghosts appear in *The Epic of Gilgamesh* and in *The Odyssey*. *The Aeneid* tells of "ghosts rejected . . . th' unhappy crew depriv'd of sepulchers and fun'ral due . . . whose bones are not compos'd in graves. A hundred years they wander on the shore." Cicero wrote of two friends traveling from Arcadia to Megara, where they stop at an inn. Late that night, one of the men has a terrible dream in which his friend appears, explaining that he is dead—that the innkeeper has murdered him and hidden his body in a wagon full of dung. Of course it turns out to be true. In *Macbeth*, the title character's guilty conscience is pricked by the ghost of his late friend, Banquo, which appears at a castle banquet. And in *Hamlet*, the ghost of the Danish prince's father asks for remembrance and revenge. Ghost stories started appearing in Chinese literature as early as the third century CE, and typically entailed lissome female spirits seducing young scholars.

But today in America, belief in ghosts is an out-there and fringey kind of thing, on par in the eyes of the nonbelieving world with ufology and the bending of spoons. *Fortean Times*, Britain's primary magazine probing what it adultly calls "the world of strange phenomena," runs stories about haunted inns and poltergeists alongside stories about giant spiders, lost continents, crop circles, herrings falling out of the sky, and women claiming to have been impregnated by aliens. The TV mediums James Van Praagh and John Edward have done well for themselves by claiming to receive messages from the dead loved ones of audience members. Their fans are devoted, but the vast majority of the public just laughs.

A hundred years ago, attempting to contact the dead was trendy. The trend began in 1849, when the adolescent Fox sisters announced to a credulous world that they were in regular conversation with the ghost of a murdered peddler in their New York home. The Fox girls asked questions of "Charley" and he answered, or so it seemed, with a series of knocks. The Fox girls became overnight celebrities, and soon thousands of would-be mediums went into business all over Europe and America. Séances were being held in private homes and crowded auditoriums—and palaces, among crowned heads. Typically, a circle of attendees sat in darkness holding hands. The medium would ask the spirits to appear and, if all went well, solid objects would rise into the air, seemingly held by unseen hands. Musical instruments played, apparently blown and stroked by unseen hands and lips. Voices emerged from nowhere—claiming to be speaking from the Other Side, an afterworld that resembled our world, but was nicer and sunnier, like summer camp.

Spiritualism became a new religion. By 1855, it officially claimed two million adherents. Daniel Dunglas Home, a star medium of the day, counted emperors, dukes, and princes among his personal friends, and his ardent champions included

the poet Elizabeth Barrett Browning. Spiritualism was so ubiquitous in late nineteenth- and early twentieth-century Europe
and America that cases are on record in which séances were
employed by detectives as part of their crime-solving techniques.
Arthur Conan Doyle was a devotee. While enroute to a speaking engagement one day, Doyle learned that his son had died of
combat injuries abroad. He kept the engagement: "Had I not
been a Spiritualist, I could not have spoken that night," Doyle
later told a friend. "As it was, I was able to go straight to the
platform and [say] that I knew my son had survived the grave,
and that there was no need to worry."

A religion based on talking with the dead was perfectly suited
to an era characterized by both romantic sentimentality *and*
amazing advances in science and exploration. In the age of
Dickens and the pre-Raphaelites, everything seemed moribund
and tragic. But at the same time, in the age of Darwin and
Edison, everything seemed possible. If two living persons miles
apart were suddenly able to communicate via telephone or come
together via transcontinental railway, then surely some new
technology could facilitate communication between the living
and the dead. Why not? Was the Other Side that much more
remote than Santa Fe?

I WANTED TO convert. Age twelve, I pored over our local
phone book searching for Spiritualist churches—finding
none, unaware that a few still existed in greater Los Angeles,
in another set of Yellow Pages. They still exist today, but for

me it is too late. The Fox sisters faked it all by cracking their knuckles, their careers flaming out in financial ruin and alcoholic despair.

IN GRADE SCHOOL, I talked other little girls into performing séances with me. It wasn't that I wanted to contact a specific spirit, as did the Spiritualists. I wasn't sentimental and hadn't lost anyone I loved. Rather I craved any contact with *any* spirit, for empirical reasons, as this would confirm my wishes and hopes, would prove my father wrong, would prove to my self-centered mind that part of me would never die.

The flowerpots and ballpoint pens and party horns we set out for the spirits never moved or wrote or blew, though Carol Finch once started screaming and her mother had to slap her face to make her stop. I was a Campfire Girl, and one summer weekend we had a campout. It was a weird time for such a merry outing, given that a few days earlier, one of the girls had lost her little sister to leukemia. That spring, we had all made gifts to be given to the sick child in the hospital: raffia flowers, macaroni bracelets painted gold. We had signed an autograph hound. On its pink ear I had written in ballpoint pen, *Now 'ear's a good wish!* Now here was Marilyn in our tent less than a week after her sister's funeral. I said, *Let's have a séance,* knowing we should not, dreading it even as I said it but unable to stop.

Who should we try to contact? I said with my awful disingenuousness. Marilyn shrugged.

Let's try to contact Jessica, she said.

We held hands in the tent and intoned *Jessica* and swayed, but nothing happened. Marilyn sat there composed, and did not cry.

As a child courting ghosts, though never meeting them, I was indulged by everyone except my father.

On vacation, walking with him alongside a canal, I burst into tears, bleating, *You're going to die someday!*

Everyone is, he said unhelpfully.

OUR HOUSE WAS the least likely in all of Los Angeles to be haunted. My parents bought it before it was built. They had picked it from a blueprint shown to them by a developer who sold them on the idea of a sleek tract with after-dinner-mint-colored houses and a school. The tract was built on empty salty sandy land that, millions of years ago, was the bottom of a prehistoric sea. Fossils studded it like nuts in cake. But no humans had ever lived on that land before the tract was built. Who would haunt such a place? The patio and porch still smelled of new concrete. I told myself maybe a roofer had died accidentally while building it, or an electrician or a plumber. Had the architect who designed the tract died just after it was done, and in his dying hour remembered ours? *I dunno why, but I just loved that one.*

I KEPT ASKING everyone whether they had ever seen ghosts. Kids at school, my parents' friends, weird strangers in Laundromats. It always came out slurred: *Have you had any uncanny encounters?* At age eleven and twelve you can just barely get away with asking such questions. Ask them as an adult and they peg you as the kind of person who believes in a grand Masonic conspiracy. Which I am not.

One day at school, during an oral report, Mike Butler told the class that long before he was born, his mother had a baby girl. One day while the baby was napping, Mrs. Butler went outside to hang the wash. She was going about her task when suddenly a voice came out of nowhere, as if through a loudspeaker, declaring, *Your baby is dead.* Dropping wet clothes, she ran inside. The baby *was* dead. These days it would be called crib death—sudden infant death syndrome, its cause unknown.

That night I called Mrs. Butler. She smoked into the phone. *My itsy-bitsy bean I used to call that baby,* she said and exhaled. *But she was never meant to be, is how I have to think about it now. God makes mistakes sometimes and has to throw out what He started and start fresh but who knows why. Could be she would've grown up and been murdered, or went blind.*

You heard a voice, I said.

A booming voice, she said.

I RECEIVED A Ouija board for my thirteenth birthday. It was the only thing I had asked for, picturing ghosts summoned by the board, descending on our tract from far and wide like farmhands harking to a dinner bell. My friend Wendy Yamamoto loved spending afternoons over the board with me in her lavender bedroom with its purple fun-fur rug shaped like a footprint. *Spirits, speak,* she said, our fingers barely touching the plastic planchette. It glided from letter to letter and number to number, spelling gibberish. *PLX IFM WT RT. Weirdarama!* Wendy said.

She said they were foreign messages. She said some of them might be Japanese. Then one day the planchette kept pointing to the same series of letters in the same order, time after time: GODOWN. I said it was two words: *GO DOWN*. A gully lay at the edge of our tract and if we went down to the bottom we would find bones or a corpse, I said. *Wrongarama!* Wendy said. She said it was not *GO DOWN* but, obviously, *GOD OWN*. Her family belonged to a new church. She said the message was a warning that *God owned* our souls and frowned on toying with the supernatural. Her fingers leaped off the planchette. It was a very New Testament year.

A few weeks later, Wendy asked if she could burn my Ouija board at an upcoming church retreat. The congregants were planning to throw certain books, records, jewelry, and toys into a fire. She was going to burn her leather belt with its hand-painted Pisces fish. I would not give Wendy the board. Nor would Wendy go with me to the gully. By the time I got around to going, months later, it was filled in and new houses were being built on top.

Something was down there. You know that, right?

SOMEONE DIED IN the master bedroom of the house where I live now. Her name was Theodora. She died in her sleep. She had no legs.

When I bought the house, no one told me this. Although real estate agents are legally obliged to disclose such details, my real estate agent forgot.

I *was* told that the house's former owner was a sweet old

lady in a wheelchair: a diabetic, a double amputee. Her live-in helper slept in the spare room, downstairs. Her son lived in another city and was selling the house because his mother had died, but it did not occur to me to ask the real estate agent how or where.

Theodora slept exactly where I do. There is only one logical place in the master bedroom for a bed. It has to do with where the windows are. She lived here for thirty-five years and was a member of the town's historical society, according to the neighbors. It was the neighbors who, assuming I already knew, told me that Theodora had died in the house. The live-in helper came to wake her up one day and found her dead. Was her death like a medieval *danse macabre*, the cowled Reaper perching on the windowsill, peering through the double glazing with hollow eyes, unfastening the latch and climbing in? Did he pat the flat place under the covers where her legs ought to have been and, waking her, announce: *Now you can fly!*

But I have never seen her ghost, nor any evidence of her. Not a whiff, not a touch. Not a rap, only peace and quiet. Perhaps because Theodora was a nice lady with no regrets. Perhaps when her time came she was ready to go. But here we presume.

Theodora has nothing to say to me. No deceased person ever has. Not my father, who warned me that he never would, though for a few weeks after his death a bluejay used to peck fiercely on my bathroom window. It was an aggressive jay, with an obnoxious chirp, and I wondered. My friend Sara can smell her late mother's perfume sometimes—out of thin air, thousands of miles from where her mother ever was. Youth-Dew, by Estée

Lauder. The first time it happened, Sara was driving her car. Out of thin air. *I was sniffing like crazy*, Sara marvels.

But no spirit identifiable as such has ever spoken to me. Not one. Anywhere. Ever. I have toured battlefields, bomb sites, the locations of massacres. I have been to Appomattox. I have been to the Alamo. I have been to Pearl Harbor. I have been to Little Big Horn. I have been to Flanders Fields. I have walked the streets of London, Berlin, Rotterdam, Cologne. Once rubble, the scene of so many violent deaths, how could these streets feel neutral now, breezes blowing along them bearing only the mild easygoing smells of rivers and pizza? I have been to Pompeii. I have been to Béziers in France, where tens of thousands of Cathar heretics were slaughtered upon orders of the pope. I have been to Donner Pass in the Sierra Nevada, where pioneers caught in a blizzard froze and starved, and the living roasted and ate the dead. This human misery, so many final moments and so many last words and last kisses and anguished farewells condensed. Yet in these places I feel nothing. I have been to a hundred Ground Zeroes, yet none of those killed in paroxysms of flame and gunfire and explosives had a single word for me. All those accumulated millions all over the world who have been lanced and gassed, who laughed and loved and then were burned, buried alive, and blown to bits—all of them kept their secrets when I came their way. If they wanted vengeance or validation, if they wanted anyone today to weep or know their names, I was only too willing, yet they made no sign. In their legions, the multitudes of dead—the plague dead and the war dead, all the persecuted and all the besieged, all the invaded and the executed and the sick, they have held out on me, all holding back, a vast conspiracy of silence.

Or could they simply be gone?

I cannot bear to think.

I have been to the scenes of murder, suicide, and scandal. Each time I expect to feel so much worse than I feel. A chill, a sudden drop in temperature, gooseflesh, hair rising on my neck, whispered words hanging in the air: but no, not one of these. I seek the stifled scream in some seemingly empty place, the fleeting blur, a vapor scuttling out of sight. But never. Nothing. I have been to Nicole Brown Simpson's driveway in Brentwood, up which out of sheer politeness Ron Goldman walked bearing her sunglasses. I have been to the West L.A. apartment where the actor Jack Cassidy (known to many of you as the father of *The Partridge Family*'s David Cassidy) burned to death on his sofa in a fire after a party, burned so absolutely that his identity had to be determined by his rings. The sun beat down through the window, benign. I have visited Marble Arch in London, site of the old Tyburn gallows, where James Boswell attended one of the many public executions that used to be held there and wrote in his diary of "the dismal scene . . . a most prodigious crowd of spectators. I was most terribly shocked, and thrown into a very deep melancholy." I felt nothing at all.

It is this nothingness that gets me, the plain stone and blood-fed earth and gas chambers giving no word, no clue. The idea of hell I can accept, though heaven would be better. Hell and heaven, if you believe, are at least places where people go. Even limbo and purgatory are *places*, if you believe. But nothingness looms far more sinister than all of those, far scarier than any ghost. For if the spirits will not speak, if they refuse to speak, if they continue not speaking to me, then someday I might have to start believing that they cannot speak. And where would that leave me? Nowhere, just as my father warned. Nowhere, forever, till the end of time.

9.

relief

ND THEN SOMETIMES you just want them to die. Because they want to die, themselves. It's what *the* want. The time is right, because they are tired and so are you because of age or illness or impatience. They want to. An sometimes even if they don't, you wish they would.

In the last two years before her father died, my friend Sherr had a routine. Twice a week she brought the baby to her parent house in the retirement village. The guard at the gate wave them through with a smile and always gave the baby a moc salute.

Her mother told Sherry about the day's activities. *I did wash. The pastor came by and chatted with Daddy.* Across the roor Sherry's father nodded in his La-Z-Boy.

Thyroid surgery at age eighty had left him unable to swallo When a feeding tube was surgically inserted into his stomac he believed it was temporary and the family let him keep thir ing that. Then one day six months later when the tube w still there, he looked up plaintively at Sherry, who was frosti

cupcakes for Easter, and said, *Just tell me the truth. I'm never going to eat again, right?*

The house smelled of sugared, shredded coconut. *No*, Sherry said. She saw it then, right there. His face went pale, his jaw slackening as if to tell the rest of his head: You won't be needing ME!

OK, he said.

The thing was, he had never been much of an eater. At family meals he had always picked at his food. His favorite snack was chips and beer and he never took the family out to restaurants. If you gave him a slice of pie or a banana he would eat it, but indifferently, and if you gave him nothing he would never ask.

But tell a man he cannot do a certain thing again and that's what he will long to do.

A few times every day a formula was syringed into his tube. It was a mixture of carbohydrates, proteins, fats, water, electrolytes, and micronutrients. He barely bothered getting up and watched whatever was on Channel 4, all day, even infomercials about rowing machines and silver polish. Sometimes when visitors arrived, he shut his eyes, feigning sleep. Sherry coaxed him to get out of his La-Z-Boy and walk with her around the village. He was perfectly able to walk. The tube was portable. Sherry felt strange saying those words, *his tube*. It came out sometimes sounding like *his hat*, a fun accessory, but sometimes like *his heart*, a dire necessity. She coaxed and coaxed and he lay staring at her from the La-Z-Boy, eyes milky, neck wobbling as he said he was tired and shook his head no.

The doctor says you need fresh air, she said.

The way he looked at her when she said that made Sherry want to run. His look said: Who cares what the doctor says? And fresh air why? To put red roses in my cheeks?

He never was a happy man. Even when he was young and healthy, he was brooding and painfully shy. She used to wonder why other dads had hobbies and he did not. Other dads fished or golfed or built things, but not him. As a boy he had hunted, but he gave it up. His life as an old sick man with a feeding tube was not much less active than his life as a healthy man who ate. Looking back on his life, Sherry saw disappointment, emptiness, and wasted time—and saw her mother living for a man who had nearly nothing to give. The novelist and poet A. Alvarez made a similar observation after the death of his father. After dreaming one night that he had persuaded his father to go for a walk on London's Hampstead Heath, Alvarez woke up in tears. "I was grieving for his death, but I was also grieving for what he had done with his life. The truth is, my father had never been for a walk on Hampstead Heath," Alvarez later wrote. "He'd spent his life in a business he didn't care for and had never been anywhere."

Striding around the living room, Sherry bounced the baby and watched Channel 4.

She acquired a habit of driving with her nails digging into the steering wheel. Its vinyl sheath was pocked with half-moon scars.

When her mother called to say he had suffered a heart attack, Sherry experienced a fleeting sense of ease. *It's over, at last.* But no—he was not dead but in critical care, barely conscious but stable.

Sherry and her sister rushed to meet their mother at the hospital. They stared together at the still shape in the bed, sheets tucked snugly under his chin. They stayed all day before the doctors said he would be moved to a regular ward, that they should take a break and come to see him in his new room after dinner.

They went out to eat—surreal, in a Mexican restaurant with bullfight posters and matador costumes affixed to its walls. Sherry drove back to the hospital alone, her mother and sister returning to the house to change their clothes.

He was conscious when she came in. The heart attack had left him very pale and when he tried to talk, words lurched out of his damaged throat sounding more like a cough. She held his hand. He slept.

The others came in just as he convulsed, nearly flying clear off the bed, and slipped into a coma.

In critical care again, he would not, the doctors said, regain consciousness. They said he would never open his eyes again. He was on life support and they could keep him there or take him off.

For two days they debated. *You talk as if Dad's already dead*, Sherry's sister snapped at her. *Well*, said Sherry, *he more or less is*.

The third day, Sherry brought the baby with her in the SUV.

Guess what, she told the baby in a singsong, as if they were going to the zoo or Chuck E. Cheese's. *We're on our way to kill my dad*. She did not cry. It was not so much that the death was sad but that the life stretching out before it had been sad. All that disappointment, all his disaffected brooding, ending now.

DEATHWATCHES CAN BE short or long. Certain enigmas we will never, ever sort out, such as: which is worse?

Short deathwatches scald you fast and leave you lying blistered on the shore. Long ones are trickier. After my father had his stroke, this question hovered, buzzing, in the air: how long is he going to last? Because sometimes stroke patients bounce right back to normalcy. I have known such patients and marvel at that miracle: there they go, driving cars and cooking Thanksgiving turkeys, and to look at them you'd never know.

Sometimes stroke patients struggle back, a hard road of recovery involving lots of therapy and partial loss, but life, at least: he is still here, and you can hold his hand, and wait as he labors to build a sentence, and he *will* build it because he has something to say. Sometimes they do not die outright but do not improve, either, and remain exactly how my father was: spastic and unable to sit up or hold anything. Raving nonsense, not making eye contact. (*Where have you put his glasses?* I demanded of a nurse. *He needs his glasses! That'll help.* But it did not.) The doctors told us that he might stay just like that for weeks months years. Or then again, at any moment now he might suffer a quick stroke-cluster that kills like a firing squad. I thought, *Am I supposed to wish for this?*

He did not bounce back, nor regain the skill to sit up or talk sense in that first week, so clearly it was going to be a slow recovery or grisly stasis or just death. And suddenly I would never again be who I was before, because he would never be who he was. Never. In a deathwatch, all that you remember from the world *before* no longer applies. Faces and voices you knew turn grotesque and the lighting skews. Cadences become taffylike. Gone are the very physics you once took for granted, cause and effect and beginning-middle-end. You recognize even your own face only through a haze, as if trying to will yourself awake. With every snatch of new clinical terminology you learn—apraxia, subarachnoid, hemorrhagic—each step you watch your shoes take in some lino hallway lit all night—you ask yourself, *What is this place?*

Food has no flavor in a deathwatch. The very air makes you ache. And all you know for sure is that this *will* end, sometime. It must. It is not forever. And like all bad temporary things—arguments, rock slides, traffic jams—it has only one bright spot: the fact that it is going to end. During other bad temporary things, you wish and wait, drumming the dashboard with your fingers in the traffic jam, rolling yourself into a ball during the rock slide. Awaiting relief. It's only natural: creatures in pain and angst beg and squeal for relief. But in a deathwatch, begging for your own relief means begging for someone to die.

You'd beg for that? You would.

As my father convulsed, widows my mother knew arrived to talk with her. It was like a secret sorority. Standing beside his bed—*rrrhurph*, he said, and *scotchisact*, almost as if he were really trying to talk, almost, and yawning in his customary two-syllable way—or in the hall or on the phone, these women who had lost their husbands, women who were members of that club, made her consider the relative pros and cons of long and short. *After Jim's accident,* one would start. And another: *When Harvey got sick . . .*

When death comes suddenly—some of them said—it is kind of a mercy, as it spares you weeks or months or years of worry and false hopes, horror foreseen, last breath and funeral imagined over and over and over, grief seeping into you like an insoluble stain, the shocking sickbed scenes, all those good-byes. Those are the benefits, if you can call them that. On the flip side, sudden death catches you off guard, to stagger blindly unable to understand, to come to terms, for years. By contrast— other widows said—slow deaths give you time to adjust. You acclimate, you wrestle with philosophy, you steel yourself for what is coming as athletes train for a tournament. Rather than vanish in a flash, the dying one does not leave you all alone all at once, does not *abandon you*, does not *run out on you*, but lingers long enough to—tenderly, with less and less proficiency—help you sort through things and tie up loose ends. But then again, you have to watch. You have to live through this. So which is worse? It comes down to the individuals involved, to who can bear what, but in this we have no choice, absolutely none.

My father loitered in that netherworld for three weeks, as rain sheeted past the window, blew away, and left the sky bright blue. Then marshmallow-fluff clouds came back and then the firing squad loaded their guns inside his head and shot.

Some deathwatches last for years, during which you acclimate to what you know is temporary, but *long*-temporary. You become accustomed in a way to seeing awful sights and hearing awful sounds, knowing that others in the real world do not see and hear them. Others, not you, might be lucky enough to live all their lives and never see or hear what you have seen and heard. And as you work and play, the knowledge of impending death ticks softly in the background of your mind. It's like a metronome, *bik, bok, bik, bok,* and it follows you everywhere, though ticking so softly that you can perform your tasks, entertain thoughts, idle at stoplights. But no matter what you do, no matter where you go, that rhythm filters through and yanks you back. *Bik, bok, remember me.* Try to forget for an hour or a day, then in the spreading silence:

Bok.

WHO WATCHES FOR a death? The dying, obviously. Their caregivers, relatives, and friends. Caregivers tell each other, and others tell them, *Take care of yourself, too, you know!* This is considered the right thing to say to caregivers and those who say it often feel quite good about themselves. Observers also like to praise caregivers for their spunk and selfless sacrifice. Caregivers are a subculture unto themselves. They die a million little deaths. But at the center of every deathwatch is the one being watched: sick but not quite *that* sick, doomed but not yet. Everyone knows. The phrase *the future* takes on a peculiar taunting meaning. So does the word *hope*. What are you hoping for? Everyone knows. It is just a matter of when. Waiting settles into your cells: you live with bated breath, hearing that metronome, shuffling as if shackled.

The one who is waiting to die dislikes being a burden, dislikes bringing others down. It is tiresome, it is embarrassing to always be the center of attention when the attention is leaden and solicitous and hopeless. Waiting to die is a bore, a worse bore knowing that others are waiting, too, whether or not they know you know. You are superfluous. You feel like the ornament of a frivolous god who displays empty shells on shelves and then forgets about them. My friend Erika remembers visiting her grandfather in the hospital after his second heart attack. She was trying to cheer him up when he took her arm and patted it. He smiled. *Stop it, don't worry,* he told her in his thick German accent. *I'm already dead.*

Because the issue cannot be forced, a deathwatch is a test of endurance for all concerned. No one is allowed to admit wanting its particular reward. If he or she who is waiting to die comes out and just admits it, his or her companions roll their eyes and say, *Tsk tsk, think positive,* and, *Is that any way to talk?* Deathwatchers are constrained never to tell the truth in public. Co-workers do not pat deathwatchers on the shoulder and say, *I wish your dad would die!* Pity comes to deathwatchers, but it usually remains unspoken because this is all so messy and shameful and nobody *really* wants someone to *die,* do they? And because the truth is lurking so close under the surface, people tend to avoid deathwatchers in general. Admire them, yes, but at a distance, because no one really wants to know.

Beatrix Potter made no secret of her wishes, writing in a letter to a friend: "My old mother is refusing to die. She was unconscious for four hours yesterday, and then suddenly asked for tea . . . we hope it will soon be over." One month later, it *was* over, and the author of *The Tale of Squirrel Nutkin* mused in another letter that her mother "was too strong, she lived after her works were worn out." Writing of her father's death, Potter was just as blunt: "We are very thankful it is over, as we feared he might drag on for weeks longer."

The end will come, which will be bad, because by definition death usually is. The end will come, which will be good, because—well, just because. When he or she dies, you get your life back. What you will feel then is relief. And grief. And shame, because you wished. And anticlimax, because nothing is ever exactly as you planned. A long-awaited death is never as clean as you thought it was going to be.

MY FRIEND MIKE was in third grade when his father was first diagnosed with cancer. After surgery and treatment, it kept coming back, and Mike spent the next eight years watching his father—*pretty much the best dad anyone ever had*, he says—die slowly. Major illness is difficult enough for small boys to comprehend, much less impending death. Mike had to know about both. *I had the classic awkward-chubby-acne-goofy childhood and adolescence*, he says wistfully, *and my dad's illness didn't help*. What was going on in Mike's house was not the sort of thing a guy can rap about with pals over a Slurpee or a game of Space Invaders. It is not the sort of thing to tell your buddy who is whining, *My dad's such a dick*. You run out of safe things to say and so do they.

The few friends I had at the beginning of high school were gone by halfway through, Mike muses, *probably on account of the death vibes coming out of me.*

Then one Tuesday afternoon in eleventh grade, a school

monitor arrived with a note from the head office summoning Mike out of class. *I was not told why but of course I knew.*

Mike's father had always promised his wife that he wouldn't die without her. On that Tuesday, he waited for Mike's mother to rush over from work, and he was true to his word. It was all over by the time Mike arrived, but for Mike that was a huge relief. *It wasn't a nice pleasant death. The cancer that had been eating him from within all that time finally bit through something he couldn't live without.* At the very end, Mike says, *there was a lot of blood, mostly of the vomited kind.*

ON THAT TUESDAY afternoon, Mike's dad gained a kind of relief, too: a liberation from being so sick for so long. The very ill endure in bodies that behave according to what seems the cruelest plan, bodies that become barely recognizable as such. My friend Wynne watched her mother sicken, year by year, with Lou Gehrig's disease. Losing one capability after another, Wynne's mother finally could "speak" only by jerking one shoulder. Wynne wondered if such suffering could possibly serve some numinous purpose. Ludwig van Beethoven began losing his hearing when he was very young—in his prime he became totally deaf. According to deathbed witnesses, the great composer's last words were: *I shall hear, in heaven.*

Sometimes death brings liberation in the most obvious sense. In the former Soviet Union, the Gulag was a brutal concentration-camp system that incarcerated millions of political prisoners. Launched shortly after the revolution, the system grew in size and ambition over the next few decades under the direction of Josef Stalin. On the dictator's whims, not only dissidents and suspected dissidents were swept up, but their entire families were persecuted as well—doomed to hunger, hard labor, and exile in icy climes. Eking out the grim half-life that Aleksandr Solzhenitsyn evokes in his novel *One Day in the Life of Ivan Denisovich*, these millions of Gulagniks hoped and prayed for the day that the aging Stalin would die. Of course they could never say so out loud, but shared glances and certain code words made their feelings clear, among their friends.

Stalin died in 1953. When this news reached the camps, the vast majority of prisoners—standing in their silent ranks for the official announcement —listened with the blank poker faces that life behind barbed wire had taught them to maintain. Others, afraid to reveal their true feelings but unable to keep still, erupted into histrionic wailing which they hoped their overseers would mistake for grief. Yet some ecstatic prisoners flung their caps into the air and shouted with joy. Around the camps in the ensuing days, the dictator's death was called a "resurrection." And, for the prisoners, it was: Stalin's death loosened the Gulag system. Within a few weeks, all pregnant prisoners were released. So were all mothers with young children. So were all prisoners younger than eighteen. Altogether, that was at least a million, with more to follow. Seldom has a death been hoped for and welcomed by so many. Seldom has one death set so many so free.

IN OUR OWN lives we erect our own prisons and climb inside, often without meaning to or without realizing that the lock will snap shut behind us. And then, because of our own cowardice, our foolish choices, our lies, and our beastliness, it comes to this: we find ourselves in situations from which we imagine only death can rescue us. Not our own deaths, of course.

Once I knew a man named Reuben Greenblatt—but here I get ahead of myself, or fall behind, because when I knew him he was not Reuben Greenblatt anymore. He had a different name. After fighting in World War II, after attending New York's City College on the GI Bill, he moved to California, where aerospace firms thrived. Once there, he realized that his hireability would be increased were he not so obviously a Jew. In a court of law he changed his name legally to Robin Greene. Of course, someone might say he still *looked* like a Jew, but if he lost his Brooklyn accent his nose might simply be seen as "prominent" and his red curls might pass for Scottish.

He began attending services at a Presbyterian church. He joined its choir and learned its hymns very quickly. At home in the evenings he read the New Testament—not that he believed in it, any more than he had ever believed anything in the Old Testament. But he needed to know the names and the parables, just in case, in casual conversation, someone mentioned Corinthians or Mary Magdalene.

That "someone" was likely to be one of the women in the choir. He had his eye on two. It was merely a matter of whether his gallant offers of rides home and his attentive smiles over coffee ultimately won over Louise or Peggy—both twenty-three and thus eight years younger than he: the standard age ratio for couples circa 1956, and both pretty, both apparently pliant, both Presbyterian.

It turned out to be Peggy, who was a receptionist at a dentist's office and whose lipstick was the paler pink and who tended a little more—but just a *little* more—toward plumpness than Louise, and who lowered her eyes and said *thank you* when he asked her to marry him.

So the community-spirited churchgoer Robin Greene, a promising new engineer at a major firm, became a model husband and, in time, the proud father of twins. One Saturday a month he volunteered at flower sales hosted by Peggy's garden club. Peggy believed he was the only child of Hector and Mary Anne Greene, a housewife and a New York bus driver, both long since dead.

Fast forward fourteen years.

The firm sent Robin—now its vice president of engineering—on a business trip. He was to meet staff members at the Defense Department and brief them on recent developments. The meeting was in Washington, but Robin thought it might be fun to leave a few days early and fly into New York. Not to see his old haunts: ancient history, to him, and his folks really *were* dead. He wanted to see New York as a first-time tourist would. He bought his tickets and kissed Peggy and the kids good-bye.

Somewhere over cowboy country, his seatmate said she hoped it would be clear when they landed, not *schpritzing*.

What I hate, she said, raking her frizzy hair with slender fingers, is *schlepping* luggage in the rain.

She spoke as if he understood the Yiddish words, which of course he did. Her name was Norma and she was a divorcée from Queens who lived in San Francisco. She asked Robin what he thought of Henry Kissinger and Philip Roth. His wife never mentioned writers to him, or politicians.

That was how he fell.

Together in New York, Robin and Norma went to bookstores, wine bars, and the theater. When she tried to bring him back to her hotel room, Robin had to steel himself and turn her down. He acted ruffled. *I'm a married man!* She scrawled her numbers on a napkin anyway, her hotel number and her home phone, then stuffed it into the pocket of his coat.

They kissed. Dry, but it lasted a long time. They kissed, then he boarded his train for Washington.

He thought the whole thing was a fluke.

Yet in the capital, he thought of her. He bought his wife and kids gifts, but he thought of Norma on her plane home, reading *Herzog* or *Catch-22*. It was not just the Jewish thing that brought her to his mind again, again, *again*, he told himself, but something about intellect, the arts, her knowing eyes.

When he got home he knew he ought to throw away the napkin, but instead he called. From work. And told her that on Wednesdays he was supposed to inspect data at a lab right near her house, yes every Wednesday, and he always took an extra hour for lunch.

Which is how it began, their years of Wednesday afternoons— in delis, at movies, in bookshops and museums. It was like their time together in New York, but transported to a strange land of lawns and sunshine and casual clothes, a land of art and intellect with borders prescribed so as to preclude running into his wife or kids or anyone they knew. Transported and ethereal and apparently endless.

Wednesday. Every Wednesday. An endless free-flowing date.

He did not sleep with her. They embraced, and they kissed, sometimes wetly. He did not sleep with her.

So that when Peggy, while trying on a dress to wear to the twins' college graduation ceremony, found a lump in her breast Robin felt guilty, but not *as* guilty as he might have otherwise. Driving his wife back and forth to doctors' appointments, canceling Wednesdays with Norma as he eased Peggy through surgery and chemotherapy, he was the model husband. Dutiful and kind.

He still *called* Norma. From his office, as he stared out the window and they talked about Jimmy Carter, François Truffaut, *Portnoy's Complaint*, Erica Jong. Sometimes Norma asked, *How is she?* Robin would say, *OK* or *Who knows* or *She has another test today.*

Sometimes he wept. When Peggy became too weak to talk and too sick to eat, he wept. Pulling diapers around her hips, he wept.

As the church organ played "Theme from *A Summer Place*" at Peggy's funeral, he wept. After the service he wept as he climbed into his car, the tears streaming down his cheeks as he sped northward, to San Francisco, faster than he'd ever driven before.

WE WISH TO be liberated from each other and from ourselves and from the past in general, from our most embarrassing moments that last like photographs in the minds of our witnesses, until they die.

My high school journalism class went on a weekend trip to San Francisco. It was a privilege, paid for by our parents: we rode a chartered bus each way and spent two nights in the Hilton, where a statewide high school journalism conference was being held.

We arrived in a happy daze after eight hours on the bus, stumbling onto the rich carpet of the lobby with its plush banquettes and a bulletin board listing all the journalism seminars to be held throughout the weekend. Right off, we saw Tommy Lasorda emerging from an elevator.

Our teacher, Mr. Durham—a pink-faced Emily Dickinson devotee who lived with his parents, belonged to a neighborhood Scrabble club, and knew my mom—told us to go upstairs and unpack in our rooms. The girls were sharing three rooms, the boys sharing four, all on the same floor. Then, he said, we must come back down and sign up for seminars. Choose as many as you like, he said, but not so many that you overtire yourselves. Spare a few hours to sightsee.

Upstairs, we unpacked. Tim Gomez unpacked a bottle of whiskey, which half of us shared, in hotel glasses with Coke from the soda machine down the hall. Then we went downstairs together, those of us now smelling of whiskey, and rather than stopping to sign up for seminars lurched outside, shambling in a large happy crowd to Chinatown. Tim Gomez bought more whiskey with his fake ID. Some touts in the street sold us theater tickets, seven dollars each, so we saw a play in which God joins a motorcycle gang and a chorus of angels sings, *You look like you're in heaven but you feel like you're in hell.* And before we knew it, it was midnight and we were rolling around in Tim's room, Tim and Rick and Vito's room, the eight of us.

And that was sort of how the weekend went, all the next day when the seminars were going on without us, into that night when some girls from La Habra High School came into Tim's room, too, with Orange Crush and Southern Comfort. The next day was Sunday and there were seminars in the morning and a convocational luncheon, which we missed, because we were throwing up. Then it was time to board the bus. The sick half of us filled the back rows—we were sick from drinking but also from arriving in San Francisco in April with only our Los Angeles clothes, our shorts and sundresses and tank tops. Now we had sore throats. The rest of our class, the sober prigs including two boys, best friends, who were planning to be priests, filled the front rows. Mr. Durham stood in the aisle as the bus pulled away from the hotel and began threading its way toward the bridge.

Well, intoned Mr. Durham, his pink face a raspberry-sherbet color, the tufts of sandy hair at the sides of his head sticking up stiffly like wings. *I can hardly find words for my disappointment.* Clinging to the overhead rail, he leaned into the back of the bus. *A waste of time, my time, your time, a waste of your parents' money—an absolute wipeout, a waste.* He wiped his palms on his pants and turned to our classmates in the front. *You, though—you ladies and gentlemen made me proud. You saw a chance to learn, and seized it!* He turned back toward us, scolding as the bus lumbered

toward the interstate. Wasting this, he said, wasting that, how
could we ever hope to have careers if we became alcoholics? He
reserved his worst fury for me. *You shock me most of all. You of all
the girls.* Was this because he had spied me in the hallway with
my dress undone? Was it because I was the features editor and
the literary-quarterly editor and the yearbook co-editor? Was it
because he knew my mom?

You, you, joining this crowd, he groaned and turned his back.
You're on my Bad List.

I was on his Bad List for two weeks. During that whole time
he kept his back to me in class and would only address me
through a third person. (*Please tell her the deadline is next Thursday.
Thank you, Kristi.*) Then I won a prize in a citywide writing con-
test and he spoke to me again, not much but a quick congratula-
tions. The school year ended. After that we saw each other only
in the hallways, and at charity events. The way he looked at me
refined itself into a gleam of ridicule (as if he saw me, then and
forever, rolling around on that Hilton bed) and scorn.

Eighteen years later my mother told me he was sick. His
diabetes had him bedridden. For two years he was home-
bound—my mother brought him bags of groceries, and
crossword-puzzle books—but then he moved into The Palms,
where he lay attached to a respirator. I felt sorry for him,
splayed out there too heavy to sit up and too blind to read,
though not sorry enough to visit him when my mother sug-
gested it. Last year he died. I did not *celebrate.* I did not *lark.* And
my classmates, the drunken ones, are very likely still alive. Yet
one witness has taken his rendering of that weekend, the one

that mattered most, with him to the grave. Which makes me happy in my monstrous way.

You might argue that, having just recounted this incident to you, I have made you my witness, too. But no, because reading a story seen through the glass of retrospect is different from seeing it firsthand, the way Mr. Durham did, before grace and years come to soften it: to say, *That was then, this is now.*

My friend Jeannette is the type who attracts devotion. You might say fixation: men and women love her, long to be around her, clamor for her jokes and observations and advice. You cannot beat Jeannette for witty comebacks or for pinpointing exactly what you thought but could not say. She is the type whom everyone calls first with news. Once you've met her, you just can't let her go.

Though she now lives far from our hometown and from where she went to college, former classmates look her up—Internet searches, phone books—more frequently than she would prefer. She finds it eerie, voices she vaguely remembers from another time and place, rattling off jokes from then as if nothing has changed, as if the Jackson Five were still the coolest band, as if she were still wearing Ditto saddlebacks, as if Space Food Sticks were the newest trendiest snack. She plays along with it, but she is shivering the whole time, drawing blanks. *What made you think of me?* she thinks but does not say. *I never think of you.*

With ex-boyfriends it has been tricky sometimes. In college she used to see a guy named Dean—a bit of an awkward setup; he was a former neighbor with only a high school diploma who drove a shuttle bus for a living, and Jeannette was a straight-A junior at a major university. They had good times, but these became fewer and fewer as Jeannette found herself having to limit her vocabulary and talk about football and cartoons when she was reading Karen Horney and B. F. Skinner for school. Finally the reach was too far and they broke up. But he still called and dropped by, and after she moved away he *still* called, for friendly chats that made her cringe, because talking with Dean reminded her of how she used to be and how she used to sound, and of the type of guy who used to attract her but not anymore. Once he even traveled a hundred miles to visit her new place. *That* was so strained, with all its elastic silences, that she thought for sure she would never hear from him again. She did, of course. He kept calling once or twice a month to update her on the go-nowhere course of his life: the bowling games, the time he got a ticket for parking in front of a fire hydrant. He tried to arrange get-togethers—perhaps he thought of them as dates—and her excuses got progressively more transparent as the years rolled on. Law school, her first trial, being made a partner in the firm, her marriage, her kids—none of this seemed to matter to Dean, who appeared incapable of taking a hint, and who stuck to Jeannette as a limpet sticks to the hull of a ship that sails to the other side of the world.

Then one day she got a call from a man who introduced himself as Dean's brother. He had found Jeannette's name in Dean's address book. He was calling everyone in the book to let them know that Dean was dead. An accident while driving with a friend. The car overturned and caught fire. Dean was paralyzed from the neck down and his legs were covered in third-degree burns. In the hospital a staph infection invaded the blisters and swept through his body. Because he was paralyzed, he felt no pain and the infection went unnoticed until it was too late. It got into his blood and killed him. Dean's brother's voice broke as he said that. The family was suing the hospital. He just wanted her to know.

She thanked him for calling. She sounded shocked, which she was, and sad. But in the back of her head was a kind of happiness. Not *unbridled joy* so much as the soft exhilaration of shutting a door safely behind you, or switching off the radio when it has been playing a song that you are tired of hearing.

Well, she thought, I'm finally free of Dean. It was a guilty liberation, and as soon as those words popped into her head she tried to blot them out. But they kept coming back. She thought of all the other people in her life—the drags, the drones, the bores, the hangers-on. She visualized each of them dying in a different way, and how free it would make her feel. She tried to blot this out as well, but she could not, and in her mind they kept driving into walls and falling off roofs, and she wondered how it would feel to have such power as to make it all come true. In the end she was glad that she did not.

AFTER MY GRANDMOTHER died unexpectedly, the question arose of what to do with my grandfather. He suffered from senile dementia, hallucinating naval scenes and circuses, and recognized us only sometimes. He mistook me for his dead sister Goldie and for a former neighbor, Larry, who robbed stores.

As a young man, Papa had been a jolly fishmonger. He had quit school at age eight, shipped out with the navy at sixteen to fight World War I, sailed home and resumed the slimy, gritty work of hauling fish at dawn from the New York docks to a shop where he gutted and filleted all day as scales made a glistening scrim on his wrists and blood tinted the ice. As the nerves in his legs began to fray and misfire—probably a rare genetic disease, but he blamed the too-tight hand-me-down boots he had been forced to wear in childhood—he started to limp, acquiring a rocking gait that in his baggy trousers made him look like Popeye. When I was six he snared a frog in a cigar box and gave it to me. He bought me candy bars and comic books: Archie and Twilight Zone and Tippi Teen. Then one day behind the familiar casing of his skin his mind began to go. I was twelve when my father said, *His mind is gone.*

Now that I was fifteen he had become a phantom trailing cigar smoke. His stogies set curtains afire and, at the table, he crunched chicken bones to paste and showed his tongue. His chiseled cheeks evoked a Cossack who raped our ancestress somewhere, sometime: his eyes, cobalt, darted after chimerical jugglers and torpedoes.

The neurological damage in his legs meant that he walked with a walker but sometimes fell to the ground and writhed like an insect, not knowing who or where he was—though, as the senile will, he rattled off his phone numbers and addresses from decades before. Before Nana died he would sit with her in their apartment bolt upright, chain-smoking Roi-Tans, watching wrestling at top volume, because he was deaf in one ear. *It's all*

rigged! he would shout. *Lookit that phony knockout, Jeezis H. Kee-rhyst.*
Nana shuddered with revulsion, smoothing her hair. Bathed
in the bouncy blue light of the TV, she stared out the window,
across Linton Street to the Bonny Basket Market. Then one day
when she had an accident she saw in it a chance to escape from
him, and willed herself to die.

I did not see her die, but I was told that when she did, Papa
let go of his walker, threw his hands into the air, and said, *OK,
you win,* his eyes blue marbles, rolling.

With Nana gone he could not live alone. Nor would my
mother put her father in a nursing home. He moved into our
guest room.

My mother looked like the mourner she was: red eyes, white
arms hanging limp at her sides. Her grief was no ordinary
grief. She blamed herself for not having realized how much her
mother had suffered, for not having helped out enough. She
blamed herself for having been carefree. Even back then you
could hire attendants by the hour or by the day to help you take
care of the old and sick, but Nana had not, and now my mother
would not. She took her father's care wholly upon herself. Of
course, he needed constant care, which is how one sorrow led
to another, like a hall of mirrors.

She followed him with a box of Handi-Wipes. He believed
Krauts were in the bathroom. She quit going to her mah-jongg
club. Our house smelled of cinnamon-spice air freshener and
smoke, and Papa muttered things in a dry warning voice such
as, *Look out—it's Clancy!*

He still had some hold on this world. The wrestling matches, and his games of solitaire, and sometimes he would catch my eye and say with the saddest look, *Can I help you in any way? I seem to have nuttin to do.* His eyes would roll. He spoke of Nana: *Can I go with Rosie?* Then in an instant he would say he had to swab the deck.

His nicotine-soaked fingers made yellow trails on walls and windowsills. He called Chinese food *chinks.* He broke your heart twiddling his thumbs. *Can I help you with something, Larry? Anything at all?*

We were prisoners with Papa. Hermits, and Mom was the most cloistered hermit of all. Dad went to work, I went to school, at the slightest chance I ran off with friends and boyfriends, a bat out of hell, a jailbreaker, a refugee, leaving her behind on the sofa in a housecoat with a cup of decaf and a magazine. She tried to make the wait even easier for me, sending me away on package tours that lasted all summer, so that I saw Canada and Trinidad, I saw Wyoming, I saw New Orleans and it looked just like part of Disneyland. I called home from hotels and felt guilty for sunbathing, far away.

HALF-DEATHS ARE THE cruelest things.

Our world as it once was was over. Travel, restaurant meals, days at the mall with Mom, all gone—and now a thousand sunny days were being wasted, bleaching the concrete of the patio. Statistics pressed against him but he lived, and in living killed those around him, but without sin and through no fault of his own. Weeks turned into four years. Sometimes he threw his hands into the air. *OK, you win.*

When I started college, he was still there. I could have chosen a school close to home, but fled to a school three hours up the coast, where fifteen thousand students were lovely and clean and young.

If you think leaving home lets you escape a deathwatch, think again. Strands of my hair still twined in the pink fibers of the bathroom rug where Papa walked, my old bed breathed my scent—I thought I had left it behind but I had not. Time and place are much more permeable than that.

In the middle of drunken parties at school or late at night while studying I would scramble for the phone and call my mother. Sometimes seven calls a day: *Hiii.* I wanted to say I am sorry I am here and you are there. I wanted her to hear the words of that song: *Any day now, I shall be released.*

I just wanted to say I know, I know.

She never carped and she never complained. She asked about my classes and my clothes in a voice as translucent as shellac. *A date? What are you going to wear?* She talked that way in January, February, and March. *Was your Spanish test hard?* She talked that way, and Papa died and she decided not to tell me.

He collapsed in the living room. Did I call that day? Surely, and she acted as if everything were normal. The next day—surely I called then, and she acted as if everything were fine. I prattled: *In anthro class we learned about a cargo cult!* Then one day she finally sighed and said, *I have something to tell you.*

How many times did I call and talk to her in that week before she told me he was dead? She said she waited a week because she thought I "couldn't handle it." She said she and Dad had talked it over and decided I should not be told yet, that I was young and fragile and in the middle of midterms. Maybe they really believed this, but I don't know. I think their secret had nothing to do with me. I think she couldn't handle Papa's death herself, at first. I think she was not absolutely certain it was true. For four years her life had been his life and his life hers. The rug was yanked out from under her feet. She was in freefall. Everything was strange.

How was that week for her? This wild succession after all the years of sameness: sirens wailing, paramedics, mortuary, cemetery, all without a word to me. My piping voice over the phone: *My roommate does this creepy thing with hamburgers. She makes a pool of mayo on the plate and dips the burger in the pool before taking a bite!* She cleaned the house, rubbed down its walls with ammonia, flung wide its doors and windows, aired the sofa cushions on the patio, rented a Rug Doctor. It was the moment she had waited for. *Ladies and gents, the moment you've all been waiting for!* But waiting for someone to die is not like waiting for the mail to come, or waiting for your birthday or a train.

In that week she wondered: Had he been happy, even just a little? Had she done enough?

Those clear March days: did their friends wonder why I missed the funeral?

The last to know: I feel in perpetuity a selfish clod, painting my nails and reading *The Teachings of Don Juan* as that day came and went, dissecting a cat in my zoology class as they slid my Papa into his tomb.

10.

horror

THE THINGS I have seen that I wish I had not:

A broken arm bone sticking up through the skin of a boy who had slipped off a jungle gym onto the concrete and was lying very still. The bone jutted up, erect, like a tusk, white streaked with red.

Catheters.

Bedpans.

Seizures.

My father, delirious—not transitorily but permanently, because his real mind would never come back: a span that lasted, mercifully perhaps, only three weeks until his death.

A man—a total stranger, copper-skinned and big—falling to the floor in a Chinese restaurant where, age eleven, I was putting the first spoonful of my noodle soup to my lips. He was having a heart attack, and died right before my eyes.

The mind is such a permeable thing. Broken bones heal. Broken skin heals—thanks to modern medical science, often without a trace. Scan my body for surgical scars and you will find none, yet the surgery was done, the incisions made, the wounds

held together with stitches and tape. Hurt the body, within reason, and it bounces back, bearing no visible marks, leaving no
trace of pain. Sooner or later you can forget that assault on the
protons altogether. But the mind. Poor mind. As soft as butter.
As impressionable as Silly Putty. Expose it to certain images,
sounds, odors, touches—thanks, five senses!—and they will be
yours for life. They become flashes, memories: the good ones
you summon at your will and for your pleasure, the bad ones
that lurch and leap unbidden back to you, again and again, and
the more you yearn to forget them, to wipe them out, rewind-
delete, the sharper and more glaringly insistent they become.
They will not let you go, horrible memories. Sometimes they
keep you up at night. Sometimes they interfere with everything.
Sometimes they even make you sick.

The good times spin and spin but life is round and round and
round she goes, and where she stops—

And life is eeny, meeny, miny mo and slot machines coming
up lemon, cherry, bell, and bar and what will be the last time I
ever see *her*, and *him*, and *them*? The good times spin. And please
please please don't let my last image of you be shocking. You
who are beautiful now. You who laughs as if you will never stop.
Please don't turn into a flash that makes me turn to someone on
the subway or at an adjacent desk weeks months years afterward
and say, like a sibyl intoning: *I've just remembered the projectile vomit-*
ing. To which she might reply:

Really? I've just remembered the car bursting into flames.

Trauma, like shock, has physiological as well as mental effects.
Trauma counselors appear at schools where shootings have taken
place or students have died by other means. They make themselves

available at workplaces struck by disaster: fires, earthquakes, murders, bombs. They were ubiquitous in New York offices after 9/11, though a *New Yorker* article concluded that this therapy was not an absolute success. Certain cities employ staffs of official trauma counselors whose job it is to visit homes where violent events such as suicides have transpired and there are survivors attempting to cope. Most of us, however, do not avail ourselves of such services because most of us—in our eyes and in the eyes of the world—simply do not qualify. We are private citizens in every sense of the word. Your tragedy was not shared by an entire student body or factory employee roster. Your tragedy was not the subject of front-page or even back-page headlines—perhaps it did not even spawn an obituary in the local paper. Your tragedy was experienced by you and a circle of other private citizens, each of whom was thrown into a certain isolation afterward by the rules of etiquette: a code of silence, a chin kept up, a cheery smile—if not *right* afterward, then soon. *Get a life and get over it.* In which case the set of events leading up to and composing your tragedy, the detailed blow-by-blow, the blood and guts of it, remains a secret from the outside world. Meanwhile it plays and plays and plays full-blast inside your mind. Poor mind.

Sometimes it helps to talk about it. Describing dire scenes can be cathartic. Witness the great literature and artworks that are no more and no less than exorcisms—disgorgements, purgings, screams. Most of us have no one to tell. At least not to tell in the depth of detail we require to flush it out, to blunt its edge, to dull the sound track just a bit. Because we would have to feel free and comfortable with this recipient of our horror. Like tar babies, our details would adhere to him or her: the sticky images and sounds we fling his or her way unasked-for, even secondhand, will cling. Imprint themselves, maybe a little skewed as in a game of Telephone, but stuck. To share our horror is not merely to burden a fellow human being but to inflict, imprint, infect.

Not all of us have dire scenes to share. Some are lucky and saw nothing at all. My friend Jamie saw his father for the last time in a hospital bed, dying of myeloma, withered and pale and looking exactly as ill as he was. *I want that image to finally go away,* Jamie says, *or be subservient to the good memories.* In a way he envies his mother, who had not seen her ex-husband since long before he was sick, and his brother, who also missed the final stages. Jamie had to call both of them long-distance and tell them the news, but the communication felt incomplete and somehow inauthentic, as if they were all on different planets. Jamie had seen the dying man, and his mother and brother had not. They were lucky and he resented that luck, because now he was branded by an image he could not shake, and has not shaken yet.

Some who never saw the worst of it say that they wish they had, or almost wish they had, because not having seen the really grisly scenes, not having seen an actual corpse, they now go through life not entirely certain that the person in question is actually dead. I know a woman whose father and mother both died suddenly of heart attacks within weeks of each other while she was traveling overseas and could not be reached. While she is grateful that her final memories of her parents are of an ordinary-looking man and woman waving happily from a departure gate at the airport, she is dogged on sleepless nights by the notion that their deaths were actually some carefully orchestrated hoax, though she cannot imagine what its motive might have been.

My friend Mike is also grateful not to have been with his father at the very end, but then Mike had watched him die gradually over the past eight years. When it became clear that the final moments were approaching, the hospital called Mike's mother at work, and she raced over in her car. *My father promised to wait for her*, Mike remembers, *and he did. I was always happy that he didn't wait for me. I was grateful to be spared that last memory. I don't think death is a good last memory to have of someone, even of a kitten.* It was a terrible deathbed scene, with much blood. Mike can picture it, and does, but takes comfort in not having seen that last bit firsthand. He saw enough firsthand, before that day, to fill a book.

After watching his father die, Robert Louis Stevenson wrote of hoping that "he will begin to return to us in the course of time, as he was and as we loved him." But for the time being, the old man remained fixed in Stevenson's mind as a "dread changeling," barely recognizable. Recounting the death of his mother, Albert Einstein spoke not as an intellectual icon but as a humble, helpless son: "One feels right into one's bones what ties of blood mean," Einstein later wrote. "I know what it means to see one's mother in torturing agony; there is no consolation. We all have to bear such heavy blows, for they are indissolubly linked with life." Such is each witness to a death the bearer of dread chronicles, and a kind of inadvertent bard. Glance into any crowd in the street: you have no idea what magnitude of misery those strangers could describe to you.

You don't want it to reflect back on the dead person. It's not his or her fault. These bad memories are not all we have of him or her, yet even one *small* awful memory has a way of crowding out twenty good or at least placid, unremarkable ones. It is as if bad memories are made of some entirely different substance than all other kinds, transmitted to the brain by different means. Last impressions are lingering impressions, good or bad, and unfortunately our last impressions are often the very worst. Jamie wonders by what science or cosmic logic his deathbed image of his father, based on an hour-long visit, still cannot be outweighed and outbalanced—three years later—by those hundreds of hours they spent together on the porch at the house in the country, listening to animal sounds and talking man-to-man under a cobalt sky where stars glittered like sugar.

Firsthand, it is all so much more vivid and more intimate. It transports you out of anonymity and into a new status: you are a witness. And like those who witness crimes, you did not ask for this, you do not like it, you yearn to escape, turn back the clock, and fade into the crowd. But you cannot. Now and forever you are a witness to a drama, the most crucial and climactic of dramas in the world. It is an honor, in a way. You are a member of yet another secret club: those who have seen horrible things. You have been gifted with an irrevocable clarity. You are experienced. There is something hallowed about this. But like initiation rites down the ages, like all ritual scarifications, this one leaves marks.

WHEN MY FRIEND Justin was eleven, his mother announced that she couldn't stand his father's loud snoring anymore. So his dad started sleeping in Justin's room. *I slept on the top of a banana-colored bunk bed in a room in the back of the house,* Justin remembered in an article he wrote many years later. *My father slept in the bunk below me.*

When my father left in the mornings he made no noise and I never woke up, never peeked, never even stirred. When morning came, I'd look down to find the bunk below empty. It was like magic. Every morning.

In the middle of one warm night soon after his dad's fifty-fifth birthday and right before Father's Day, *I heard something loud from below and it was my father's snoring again. I punched my pillow and yelled, "Shut up."*

The snoring got so loud it shook the wooden bed. I rolled over on my stomach and pulled my pillow over my head really hard . . .

When morning came, I awoke on my back. I could see the white specks of asbestos on the ceiling. Like cottage cheese. Or the moon's surface . . . but something was not right; I could feel it. I wasn't alone.

Justin eyed the clock across the room. It was 8 AM, long after his father usually left the house. He swung his head over the railing to look down at the bottom bunk.

My father's eyes were open slits, his mouth wide open. Yellow teeth, gold cavities. He wore a white V-neck T-shirt. Curly chest hairs. Boxer shorts. Hairy legs . . . I jumped down from my bunk. I got on my bare knees and knelt next to him. If you want to check if someone is dead, I'm thinking, put a mirror up to their mouth. I saw it on TV. I shook his body.

"Dad?"

One day, years before, Justin had asked his father to describe the grossest thing he had ever seen in his entire life. A dead body, his father had said. How did you know for sure that it was dead? Justin had asked him. His father said: I touched it, and it was cold.

Now Justin laid one hand on his father's face.

Cold.

I put my ear on his chest and shook him by the arms. "Dad? Dad?"

He ran to get his mother. She was getting dressed, still clad only in underwear.

I think Dad's dead, the boy said, and standing there in her panties she screamed.

It had been a heart attack. Later that day, the two of them stood looking at the corpse. It lay on a gurney, draped to the shoulders in a white sheet, head propped on a cushion, hair combed back. Justin's mother used the palm of her hand to lift her husband's eyelids. She wanted to see how blue his eyes were, to show her son how blue they were.

My father's eyes were like polished blue rocks, Justin remembers, *looking straight up into the light.*

WHAT MAKES HORROR horror is that it is so unpredictable. Even if you try to prepare for it, you will always be caught off guard, if not by the spectacle itself, then by its magnitude or by how it really feels. Living in a college dorm full of girls at age eighteen, I developed the perverse conviction that one day I would walk into our large shared bathroom and find one of my hallmates dead. I would open a toilet stall—I was sure—and see someone slumped over, dead of a brain hemorrhage or with a syringe sticking out of her arm. I couldn't predict *who* it would be, but I felt so certain it would happen that I got the chills every time I entered the room, especially if it was quiet and if it was the middle of the night. As it happened, one of the girls *did* die, but not in the bathroom. No amount of timorous tiptoeings across that cold tile floor could have prepared me for what fate really had in store.

Even when you think you are prepared for the worst, somehow you are never quite ready, you can never steel yourself enough or breathe deeply enough or talk yourself through it ably enough not to be floored, knocked out, repulsed. The world has so much in it that we never in our normal *before* lives even realize exists. So much hidden behind the smooth and shiny surface: roiling, grotesque, awful things that will be revealed to us one by one—then we will rue not having savored that smooth shiny surface back when it was all we saw.

In his four-volume series *Barefoot Gen: A Cartoon Story of Hiroshima*, Keiji Nakazawa, an atomic-bomb survivor, relates the largely autobiographical tale of a seven-year-old Hiroshima boy who experiences the events of August 6, 1945, and their aftermath. Nakazawa sets the morning of August 6 against a backdrop of rising-sun flags fluttering above depleted fields as victory verses are sung by starving townspeople. As the day begins bright and hot, young Gen wends his way to school pondering boyish trivia while his hardworking father, pregnant mother, little brother, and elder sister get ready to start their daily routines at home. A woman stops Gen on the street to ask for directions, then everything fades to white in an instant. We see something falling, Gen's arms flying up to protect his face, a house exploding into splinters and glass shards. Protected from the explosion's

4,000-degree heat by a cement wall behind which he happens to be standing when the bomb falls, Gen stands up and brushes himself off only to discover that the woman to whom he had been talking moments ago is dead, her face melted like cheese. Gen shouts to a passerby, asking the man to help him care for the burned woman, but then he realizes that the man's face is melted, too, his trousers burned off, his buttocks and privates bare, skin hanging in gory strips from his back and arms. Gen witnesses a town transformed, its familiar skyline razed, and the baffled boy cries for his mother.

Nothing would ever be the same again, for the cartoon character or for the real boy who would grow up to be the cartoonist. In rapid succession, Gen has just been forced to leap through several momentous psychological hoops. Having survived a terrifying explosion, he comes to his senses only to encounter a corpse, and not just a corpse but a grossly disfigured one. Seeking aid in dealing with this shocking prospect, this corpse at his feet, he realizes that no aid will come. Calling for aid but receiving none, he looks around and sees that the reason he will get no aid is that everyone as far as the eye can see, alive or dead, is injured beyond belief. In an instant, Gen has become a member of the subculture that would forever afterward be known in Japanese as *hibakusha*: atomic-bomb survivors. Never was a distinction more unwanted by so many. Because it is so visual and provides the most primal kind of reading experience, the comic-book format is perfectly suited to this tale of real-life horror. In box after box, on page after page, Nakazawa renders images that bring the disaster more jarringly alive than mere words ever could. Gen rushes home to find his father and siblings pinned under their fallen house. They are alive, but injured and stuck—and even together, Gen and his mother do not possess the strength to lift the fallen roof beams. A fire is racing through the neighborhood and Gen's father urges them to save themselves, to run. They do, encountering death every-where: roasted corpses on land, bloated corpses clogging the river, vaporized victims reduced to human-shaped shadows on the pavement. Soon many of the living start to die of their injuries and of radiation sickness as well, before Gen's eyes. As we follow the boy through the coming months, we watch him mature rapidly, becoming hardened and wary but also generous and clownish, as if—having recoiled and recoiled and recoiled more in a season than most of us do in a lifetime—Gen is now determined to overlay the awful images in his head with as much joking and singing and kindness as he can.

Thirty years after experiencing the bomb, Nakazawa was still wrestling with those images. Because his trauma was part of a major apocalypse with global ramifications, and because he was a skilled comic artist, he was able to make something of it that, he dearly hoped, might help heal and change the world. In his introduction to the series' final volume, Nakazawa explains: "I did not write *Gen* simply to decry the destruction of the atomic bomb. I wanted to portray the process by which the people of Japan were caught in the grip of a system of imperial fascism . . . that thrust the nation into a war of aggression. . . . I wanted [the next generation] to know about the atrocities that Japan com-mitted in China, Korea, and the rest of Asia." Horrific as the scenes of death and destruction were, the series put them into a context larger than Hiroshima-as-target, as Nakazawa crosscut to scenes of ruthless Japanese bombing campaigns in the South Pacific and of officers brutalizing trainees at kamikaze camps. The result is a passionate but universal antiwar entreaty. Nakazawa might never have been spurred to start the series were it not for yet another horrific image that he encountered more than twenty years after the bomb. As he explains in the introduction to the final volume, his long-suffering mother survived radiation sickness but was in constant ill health until her death in 1966. "When her body was cremated," Nakazawa recalls, "I discovered . . . nothing was left of her bones. Usually [fragments of] bones remain after cremation, but radioactive cesium had eaten my mother's bones away, and they had turned to ash. The A-bomb had taken everything from me, even my precious mother's bones. Rage boiled up inside me . . . I was seized with a desire to write about it."

Because his horror and rage and desire are part of a bigger picture, he was able to transform them into a work aimed at creating a better future. What, on the other hand, can we do with ours? Especially if we cannot write or draw?

Just for ourselves, if not for anyone else, we can do this: Let those horrors be a constant reminder of how bad life can be, so that *any other time*, when we are experiencing *anything short of horror*, we should be grateful and glad, knowing it could be so much worse. You will not whine about slow checkout lines or dry flyaway hair if you remember how it felt to take someone off life support or see a mangled human form at the bottom of a cliff.

. . .

SOME OF THE worst images of death that will ever imprint themselves on your mind might be those that you happened upon by accident. The dead person was not someone you knew but a total stranger. You become a witness—upholding the sacred task—for someone who never even saw you, or with whom you never exchanged a word. My friend Kit was acquainted with the two men who committed suicide in his house a week apart, but only barely. And he didn't like either of them. They were obnoxious and thoughtless while alive, then their deaths left him with memories grislier than most of us are ever likely to incur. One of them overdosed on heroin, falling face-down and shattering his nose on the bathroom floor before two housemates arrived home hours later and found him dead. The other shot himself inside a locked bedroom. He was not technically a resident of the house but a semipermanent houseguest, the boyfriend of a resident, and someone else was home at the time and heard the shot. For hours that afternoon, cops and paramedics and finally the coroner trooped up and down the stairs. Kit was standing with a large group of housemates and neighbors when the black body bag was carried down the stairs. *I was pissed off. I thought: Dude, you've got a home of your own. If you were gonna snuff yourself, why not do it there?* The coroner was the last to leave, and the rest of the crowd trailed away into the night. Kit and one housemate were sitting alone on the staircase. *Joe said, This is a hell of a day. I said, Yeah. Then it hit us both at the same time: The bedroom was full of blood.*

Neither rescue squads nor police departments nor coroners clean up after violent crimes and suicides that occur in private homes. It's not their job. Usually the task falls to independent contractors that specialize in this service. Kit and Joe couldn't afford to hire professional cleaners, so they went out to a nearby free clinic and collected handfuls of plastic biohazard bags. Back in the house, they climbed the stairs with the bags and a few small plastic shovels. *There was this lake of blood and brain matter—a lake about three feet wide on the hardwood floor.* Luckily the room wasn't carpeted. They began scooping with their shovels. The brain matter looked a bit like scrambled egg. *At one point I thought, These are Cisco's brains,* Kit says. *But that's all I remember thinking.* Cisco's girlfriend, who lived in the house, was out of town that weekend. Friends called to tell her the news, and she never came back. *She never set foot through that door again,* says Kit. It struck him as more than ironic that the dead man's girl-friend—she who had known him so well, who had whispered into his ears and tenderly cradled that head who knows how many times—was spared the whole spectacle. *I barely knew the guy,* says Kit, *and what I knew about him was irritating.* Yet it is Kit who has this tale to tell, and whose fingers know a certain slippery sticky feeling that they may never feel again but which he will never forget.

SOMETIMES WHAT WE have undergone, what has imprinted itself on us, was not visceral in nature but emotional. The sound of my mother sobbing after my grandmother died: a lowing sound you might associate with bison. The disbelief in the faces and voices of those people in the Chinese restaurant who had been sitting at the table with the man who fell.

He was not Chinese, the man—no one in the Rickshaw except the cooks and waiters was. It was a busy night, a winter night but warm inside, our white teacups throbbing pink from the flashing neon on the five-and-dime across the street. Jasmine tea steamed in the cups, soup in the bowls. My mother was dragging a fried shrimp through a blot of Chinese mustard when the man rose to his feet, pushing his chair back.

It was not the sort of gesture you would notice, normally. A man neither very old nor very young wearing white trousers and a blue sport shirt and deck shoes rising in a restaurant. Perhaps he was getting up to pay the check, or to go to the men's room, or to ask a waiter a question. His chair jerked back, its unsheathed metal feet scraping the red linoleum. Pushing off from the table with the heel of his hand he took two steps, three at most, clutched his chest and groaned and crumpled to the floor.

Everything went stock-still but this. He lay, legs splayed, clasping his chest, heels plying the air as if he imagined himself climbing. All the groans I had heard in my whole life until then were fake, they were play groans in games of cowboys and Indians, or they were on Halloween sound-effects albums. The man groaned and this was real, a noise torn from the throat. Then in a slow-motion growl, from the floor, he bellowed, *Hearrrrt attack.*

How weird, I thought, for him to say it, like a person in a children's TV program who narrates his own activities. *Now I pick up my watering can and water my garden!*

One of the two women seated at his table started screaming. Another man leaped up and seized the telephone on which the restaurant staff received takeout orders. A waiter dashed out the door and started trying to flag down a police car. Cooks ran out of the kitchen, holding cleavers and spoons. A crowd buzzed around the fallen man. They raised him by the armpits—saying *one two three, go* because he was heavy—until he was half-sitting against the wall. It was probably then that they undid his shirt. Gray hair surged from his suntanned chest like smoke, so many fingers on so many different hands searching under it for a pulse.

We did not move. My mother sat with the shrimp halfway to her mouth, her elbow bent. Dad had not finished licking his lips, and they shone with pork fat as if glossed. In my hand was a soup spoon, a Chinese one with a dragon painted on it, like a party favor. Everyone else in the restaurant was rushing, shouting. We sat frozen. It seemed wrong to drink the soup from my spoon. But pouring it back into the bowl seemed wrong, too, like a sinister symbol in a movie.

The crowd hunching over the man spoke in voices shrill and shocked and baritone, the way men often sounded in our town, skippers and sports coaches and Scoutmasters and drunks. *Is it beating? Can you feel—? Sure, of course! Well—. No? Yes? Get the hell off and lemme try.* He had been dining with two women and another man—two couples? four siblings? One of the women sank to her knees pleading, *Honey? Honey?* as the other woman (her sister? her friend?) stood and crossed herself.

Their windbreakers dangled over the backs of their chairs, sleeves swinging every time someone rushed past. The sleeves looked merry if you did not see the rest.

I recognize her, my mother said, jutting her chin toward the kneeling woman. *That's Sheila from Sheila's Flower Shoppe.*

I thought, How awful. That lady spends all day—maybe today even—in a pinkblueyellowredwhite fairy-bower world of pretty scents and tissue paper and ribbon, with happy customers choosing bouquets and corsages and boutonnieres for parties, proms, and weddings. And now finds herself, come evening, in the unhappiest situation on earth.

The man was silent. All around him the flurry went on. Someone said, *I hear sirens* as the ice cubes melted slowly in the water glasses on his table, sauce congealing in the plates.

They're coming, someone said, *coming to help you*, and they stroked his head and patted his knee but he made no sound. Since saying *heart attack* he had made no more sound or movement than a stuffed toy on the floor would.

Can you feel—? He seems cold.

The kneeling woman seized his wrist, bent closer, put her cheek to his.

Honey?

II.

irreverence

WHEN THE MATRIARCH gorilla at a Chicago zoo died in December 2004, its companions performed what the zookeepers called a "gorilla wake." One by one, the surviving apes left the open air of their enclosure and filed purposefully into the building where thirty-year-old Babs lay dead. The first gorilla to enter the building was Babs's nine-year-old daughter, followed by Babs's forty-three-year-old mother. The older gorilla sat beside the corpse holding its hand and stroking its belly, then laid her head on the dead arm. The other apes followed, methodically sniffing and touching the corpse. Another female brought her baby into the building and held it out as if giving Babs one last look. The apes stayed in the building with their dead matriarch for half an hour, then filed out and resumed their daily routine. The head zookeeper told a reporter that gorillas in the wild are typically known to pay respects to their dead in a similar fashion. In Africa, the primatologist Jane Goodall once observed an infant gorilla whose nearly severed arm "was about the most ghastly thing I've seen in a long while." For several days after the creature died, Goodall watched its mother "carrying the body, hitting away the flies that seethed all over it." And long after that, "still she sits and stares and stares at one or other of the other infants." Similar behavior has been noted among chimpanzees and baboons. And in humans since the dawn of civilization. In fact, this is how some archaeologists date the dawn of civilization: that point in prehistory at which the tomb, the grave, the niche, the cave was marked with signs of care, of some accompanying ritual over the dead. Current estimates set this moment at between 35,000 and 130,000 years ago. One example of a prehistoric burial was discovered at Dolní Vestonice in what is now the Czech Republic, where excavations revealed three Cro-Magnon skeletons who had been carefully posed in a grave 26,000 years ago, wearing masks adorned with pierced fox teeth.

A behavior so pervasive in human and primate societies must surely be in some way instinctive. Yet what evolutionary purpose could mourning possibly serve? Being wired for sex and combat, competition and escape, makes perfect sense. But what good could it do apes and our ancestors, or us, to mark the end of life, to be humbled before the dead?

Becoming keenly aware of the difference between life and death—the look, feel, and smell of the crossing point—attunes the living to the value of staying alive. Ceremonializing death means facing up to it, and thus facing our own mortality. Every death we encounter is a wake-up call. In every corpse we see a preview of our own. Mourning, then, is a multipurpose rite: we mourn the lost one while mourning ourselves, preemptively. While sobbing out our sorrow, we also sob out our mortal fear. We do not want to be next and we will do whatever it takes to avoid that. Grief hones the survival instinct.

We are wired to mourn. We are wired to idolize and canonize and fall to our knees grieving for the powerful but gone. We feel the tide of history rushing on and we want to be swept up in it. We long to be part of the changing of the gods.

OUR ANCESTORS DIED so easily. They knew the look, smell, and *sound* of gases and fluids bursting from the bodies of their own beloved. The corpses of men they had kissed. Of women they had courted. Of babies they had borne and taught to walk. Of siblings from whom they were once inseparable. Life was so fragile then. Wars. Epidemics. Massacres. Plagues. Childbirth. Accidents. Bacteria whose names you do not know today but which wiped out whole legions. Fevers that no one knew how to cool. Infections that you would dispatch now with soap and water raged back then through bloodstream and heart and brain. Born in the autumn of 1918, the great influenza epidemic claimed tens of millions of victims worldwide within a few months. The simplest things mowed down our forebears. Dog bites. Mosquito bites. Flea bites. Not knowing how to swim. Tragedy skulked in every field, in every room. Describing the city of Florence during the Black Plague outbreak of 1348, Giovanni Boccaccio wrote: "Many dropped dead in the open streets by day and night . . . whilst a great many others, though dying in their own houses, drew their neighbors' attention to the fact more by the smell of rotting corpses than by any other means . . . bodies were here, there, and everywhere." For Boccaccio, one of the most unnerving effects of this calamity was that, while it lasted, "there arose certain customs that were quite contrary to the established tradition." For instance, it became "rare for bodies . . . to be accompanied by more than ten or twelve neighbors to the church, nor were they borne on the shoulders of worthy or honest citizens but by a kind of grave digging fraternity newly come into being and drawn from the lowest orders of society." To him, ten or twelve was an outrage. My father had five. I know of many now who had none.

Societies—tribes, clans, towns—practiced funerary rites that were conformist but cathartic. These were acts of reverence hallowing the dead, enshrining them. Rendering them hard to forget: Iron Age Scythians in what is now Eastern Europe displayed their grief by slicing their ears, ripping their noses, and driving arrows through their hands. Polynesian islanders in mourning shaved their scalps and slashed the bared flesh with seashells until it bled. Until the practice of suttee was outlawed in 1829, many a new widow in India died on her husband's funeral pyre. In Confucian China and much of Africa, ancestor worship thrived: your dead were gods. The Warramunga of central Australia stabbed *their* scalps with sharp sticks and severed their thigh muscles with knives. Life was hard in times of yore. It was hard to give life, hard to be born, hard to persist. But so easy to die. No wonder funeral rites were hard as well. Stabbing your hand or slicing your thigh honed your cognizance of *what we stand to lose.* And of *what we do for our own. What our kind does.* The past linked to the present and the future, with this solace: *And someday this will be done for me.*

GRIEVING IN PUBLIC means having one foot in the dark and one in the light. Illusions, niceties, daily decorum shear away, leaving you free to scream. The night D. H. Lawrence died, his widow Frieda sat up with the corpse, singing his favorite German lieder, English hymns, and Scottish folk songs at the top of her lungs until daylight. Barriers fall as in those moments— slashed, stabbed, shorn—you face fate and humanity and God or gods. As billions did before, you face fear and the razor slice of love. Your days of lamentation, all-night vigils with corpses, the tombs so monumental as to last thousands of years: thus our ascendants made their farewells. Those moments, wretched and glorious, fling you to the brink. Life, death. You, I. Now, then. Never, forever. Performing those rites with your own hands, with your own voice, on your own feet, you know without a doubt that you are swinging on the gates of eternity.

WE HAVE WORKED it now so that we hardly ever have to swing on them at all and are not sure where they are. Thanks to medical miracles, sanitation and nutrition and a million other wonders, we have created a safe sparkly world that our ancestors would not recognize. We have worked it so that we don't even want to *think* about death, and we usually don't have to. Now that human life expectancy is higher than ever, you stand a good chance of reaching adulthood without ever having suffered a single close personal loss. In young adulthood, it starts—usually with grand-parents, but in these estranged days when we worship neither ancestors nor age in general, grandparents mean less than they once did. My friend Kent remembers losing his grandmother, a longtime Alzheimer's patient: *I don't think I even shed a tear,* he says. One does not feel compelled to mourn even the most obvious candidates. My mother-in-law, an only child, chose not to attend her father's funeral because she felt—as a grown woman with kids of her own by then—that her bond with him wasn't worth a cross-country trip. A professor of my acquaintance received a call recently from a detective in another state informing him that his brother, formerly one of the world's top research scien-tists, had died in a motel room under mysterious circumstances. The body was in police custody and would be released pending investigation. *Isn't that weird?* the professor mused. Weird? He gave a nervous laugh. I asked whether he was planning to fly out there to oversee the investigation and eventually bury his brother. Another nervous laugh. *Why? My niece and nephew are adults; they can deal with it.* Two months later I saw the professor again and asked about his brother. *No news,* he giggled. *He's still on ice!*

In this era of moral relativism—when it is hammered into our heads that there is no such thing as objective right or wrong—respect, much less reverence, is no longer required for the living. Nor, perforce, for the dead. Google the phrase *i hate my mother* and it yields 996 hits. *I hate my mom* yields 892. *I hate my father* yields 748; *i hate my dad* yields 808; *i wish my dad would die* yields 44; *i wish my mom would die* yields 36. I am an only child, so I don't know: is it weird that *i hate my sister* yields 4,170 hits?

If my mother-in-law ever regretted skipping her father's funeral, she never showed any sign of it. She barely spoke of him at all. By contrast, she always marked the anniversary of her *mother's* death with ritualistic gestures, rallying her children to hear somber reminiscences that they all knew by heart.

It wasn't that she hated him. It was just that she made a choice: enshrine the memory of one parent while consigning the other to a distant and much less sentimental place. But did she owe them both the same obeisance? What exactly do we owe the dead? What does it signify about us when we do more for one of them than for another? What does it say about us when we do nothing for them at all? Are we more callused than our ancestors? Do the dead know the difference either way?

We live in individualistic times. Some would say narcissistic times. We talk possessively about *rights* and *entitlements*. We are all auto-oracles, asking ourselves constantly *how we feel*.

WHEN YOU GOOGLE phrases beginning with *i hate*, most of the hits lead to blogs, chat rooms, and message boards packed with posts such as this one:

Nothing inspires a deeper feeling of nausea in me like the word "Grannie." I hate my grandmother. Really, I do. My father's mother . . . should have been drowned after she gave birth. . . . One of her favorite activities when my dad was young was to take all of the dishes out of the cupboard, break them & then blame her 4 kids so that my grandfather would beat them when he got home. . . . There are other tales of course, but they are too numerous to list in one post. Maybe I will save them up for her funeral. I was soooooo happy to hear that she was having heart problems. I practically danced when she went in for a quadruple bypass. I am going to wear a bright lime green sundress & dance on her grave. My problem is the bitch just won't die.

Did our ancestors loathe their grandmothers? Surely some of them did. Surely they were, as we are, sometimes conflicted. Unresolved. Ambivalent. But when life itself was an ongoing crisis, subsistence depended on belonging. A group whose adults rear filial children allied with their peers is a group equipped to defend itself against invasion and erosion and rot from within. No matter how they really felt, our ancestors could not afford to skip a funeral—much less muse as one writer does online:

My dad . . . he's been talking about suicide lately, and he mite die, I don't care. . . . To tell you the truth i hope he dies right now.

 And another, on another site: i hate my mom . . . i wished that she died . . . she treats me like a slave. . . . i remember one time she borrowed money from me and i asked for it later on and she said sum stuff and then she was like i should've dumped you in the trash can. . . . i hate her with all my heart . . . just cause she gave birth to me doesn't make her my mom, she doesn't act like a mom and honestly, i don't consider her my mom. . . . i know some of you guys will say you can't hate your mom, it's a phase, but truely, i hate her and i will always hate her.

 And another, on another: I hate my mother to a point where I wouldn't cry if she died, I would laugh at her funeral, I would step all over her grave, then leave her sorry ass 6 feet under.

. . .

Nᴏɴᴇ ᴏꜰ ᴍʏ friend Kent's neighbors know he never wept for his grandma. But if they knew, it's not likely that they would even care. They wouldn't banish him. Our nation's future does not depend on whether Kent cried or not. Or does it?

We're still wired to mourn. It is not as if evolution has brought us to some stark postmodern point at which we have forgotten how to love, revere, or grieve. But these are choices now.

We are still wired to face the abyss and ask what it wants of us. Still wired for the profound.

Wʜᴀᴛ ʜᴀs ʙᴇᴇɴ done for the dead that we no longer do?

It took seventy days to make a mummy: heart, liver, and other vitals excised, body cavity washed with wine, applications of honey and salt as preservatives, an elaborate binding in yards of cloth with charms and jewels inserted into the folds. In ancient Rome, the corpse was displayed for as long as a week, then carried to the cremation place in an evening parade featuring musicians and relatives bearing masks resembling the faces of those who died before. The ancient Romans had a two-week holiday every February, Parentalia, devoted to honoring deceased ancestors. Hawaiian islanders dashed out their front teeth with stones, scarred their flesh with burning twigs, and sometimes even sliced off their ears well into the nineteenth century. The missionary William Ellis wrote of seeing Queen Kamamalu having her tongue tattooed after the death of her husband, King Liholiho. Asked whether it hurt, the queen told Ellis: *The pain is indeed great, but the pain of my grief is greater.* Members of the Warí tribe of western Brazil roasted and ate their loved ones' corpses, considering it the ultimate act of tenderness—a kinder fate than the cold and loneliness and putrefaction of the filthy ground. Burial seemed barbaric to the Warí, who were horrified when government agencies forced them to start doing it in the 1960s. *Xiram pa' wiriko ko mi' pin na, je para kao inon,* one tribe member told a visiting anthropologist: *I felt sorry for he who had died; that's why I ate him.* The flesh was eaten even if it made the mourner sick, even if it was putrescent after lying outdoors during three days of ceremonies.

The Victorians and their American counterparts were obsessed with death. Its colors and symbols saturated art, spirituality, and daily life in an era marked by soaring infant mortality, epidemics, pandemics, and bloody conflicts—the Civil War turned eighty thousand women into widows in Alabama alone. A whole genre of fiction was dubbed "consolation literature." Further streams of books and articles advised millions on funeral etiquette and mourning fashion. In 1901, *Collier's Cyclopedia and Compendium of Profitable Knowledge* outlined the standard widow's wardrobe, distinguished by its use of black crape, a fabric prized for its mournful matte surface:

> *One dress, either a costume of Cyprus crape, or an old black dress trimmed with rainproof crape. . . . One bonnet of best silk crape, with long veil. . . . One black stiff petticoat. . . . Widows' cuffs, made in lawn, should be about nine inches long. . . . Young widows wear chiefly the Marie Stuart shape, but all widows' caps have long streamers. . . . If in summer a parasol should be required, it should*

be of silk deeply trimmed with crape, almost covered with it, but no lace or fringe for the first year. Afterward mourning fringe may be put on. A muff, if required, would be made of dark fur or of Persian lamb. . . . No ornaments are worn in such deep mourning, except jet, for the first year.

After that first year:

Mourning cap left off, less crape and silk for nine months (some curtail it to six), remaining three months of second year plain black without crape. . . . At the end of the second year the mourning can be put off entirely; but it is better taste to wear half mourning for at least six months longer; and, as we have before mentioned, many widows never wear colors any more, unless for some solitary event, such as the wedding of a child.

The death of each different relative required different styles:

Black, without crape, for one month is suitable in case of death of parents-in-law; after one month black and white, with lilac, should follow. For Grandparents, simple black without a touch of crape, worn for three months, is the rule. . . .

For Sisters or Brothers, six months' mourning is usually worn. Crape for three, plain black for two, and half mourning for one month; the same sort of stuffs, the crape being put on in keeping with the style of the day; bodice, crape trimmed; jacket or cape, crape trimmed; bonnet of crape with feathers or jet, hat of silk and crape. Veil of hat with crape tuck, hose black silk, Balbriggan or cashmere, handkerchiefs black bordered. Silks can be worn after the first month

*if trimmed with crape. For Uncles, Aunts, Nephews, or Nieces, crape
is not worn, but plain black, with jet for three months. For Great
Uncles or Aunts, mourning would last for two months without crape.
For Cousins, six weeks are considered sufficient.*

Séances drew eager crowds. Queen Victoria, garbed in
black for forty years and dubbed "the Widow of Windsor,"
made an international fashion of public grief. Beloved corpses'
hair was used to fashion framed pictures: blond wisps forming
a willow over a rippling auburn brook. Portraits of the dead,
sketched or painted with the corpse as a model, took pride of
place in homes. Funeral guests used beautiful lachrymatory:
little bottles for collecting their tears. Nineteenth-century cem-
eteries were monumental in design, crisscrossed with broad
shaded avenues where visitors were meant to linger long. A
popular fixture for new headstones was a bell attached to a
chain leading down through the ground and through a hole in
the casket to a ring worn on the finger of the person inside. On
the slim chance that he or she had been accidentally buried
alive, the bell could be rung upon the regaining of consciousness to alert passersby.

The dead were far but also near. And they were everywhere.
In *The Adventures of Huckleberry Finn*, Mark Twain described a
girl typical of the times: fourteen-year-old Emmeline Granger-
ford copied obituaries from the newspaper into her diary, and
painted picture after picture of mourning women. In that era,
grief *was* popular culture. Bereavement poetry peppered household magazines. In May 1856, *Harper's* ran a poem that began:

I wish that when you died last May,
Charles, there had died along with you
Three parts of Spring's delightful things

And another that began:

The night was dark and stormy, the wind was howling wild,
A patient mother watched beside the death-bed of her child. . . .
As she offered up a prayer—in thought; she was afraid to speak
Lest she might waken one she loved far better than her life.

In his most famous poem, "The Raven," Edgar Allan Poe—
who lost his beloved wife, whom he had married when she was
thirteen, to tuberculosis twelve years later—lamented *the lost*
Lenore . . . the rare and radiant maiden whom the angels name Lenore. His
narrator in another poem curses the cold sea wind that killed
his beloved:

And the stars never rise but I see the bright eyes
Of the beautiful Annabel Lee;
And so, all the night-tide, I lie down by the side
Of my darling, my darling, my life and my bride,
In her sepulchre there by the sea—
In her tomb by the side of the sea.

In 1901, *Collier's* made this prediction: "The old custom of
wearing decent mourning for those taken away from us, will
never be really discontinued in America, for it is one of those

proofs of our home affections which can never be done away with without a loss of national respect."

AND WHAT DID I wear? Less than a hundred years later, what did I wear? For my grandmother, black for three hours: for the funeral and that was all. For my grandfather, no black for anything and certainly not for his funeral because I missed his funeral because no one had told me he was dead. For my father, a black dress picked out at a thrift shop a few hours before the immurement, with a black scarf from Mom's bureau which made her cry because he had bought it for her—I didn't know—in Mexico dozens of years before, possibly on the very day I was conceived. What did I wear after that? Pink, gray, plaid, polka dots, whatever. Looking at me, you would never know. One morning three months after he died, I put on a long black coat and it came to me like a bolt: Black. Coat. A certain kind of butterfly was the most common in our tract when I was small: big black velvety wings edged with pale dots. When I asked Dad what this species was called, he said: *the mourning cloak.* I thought he said *morning.* A certain kind of bird was the most common in our tract when I was small: sleek, small head jerking as it cried *Woop! Woo. Woo. Woooooo.* When I asked Dad what this species was called, he said: *the mourning dove.* I thought he said *morning.* What a shock to learn later from books that butterfly and bird, our constant companions once, were named not for new days but for the end, not hope but misery. Staring down at the coat—vintage, wool, with big buttons, slit in back—I thought, *So this is it, the mourning cloak.* But I was not wearing the coat to mourn him, and I knew it. I was wearing the coat because it was cold. And all that day whenever I glimpsed my reflection I felt like announcing, like a medieval flagellant: *Ladies and gentlemen, I might seem to be honoring my father but the color of this coat is sheer coincidence.*

Do I still love him? Yes. Do I want to forget him? No. Am I in denial? No. Is his grave fifty thousand miles away? At the top of a mountain? At the bottom of the sea? No. Am I a rationalist for whom all rites are anathema? No. I like rites. Am I afraid of graveyards? No. I have visited dozens of them, those of strangers, for amusement, on vacation, for something to do.

YET THERE HE lies, or whatever is left after ten-plus years: which no one wants to picture. There lies what passes for him, right off a major freeway in a metropolis, ten feet off the ground, behind his plaque which in ten-plus years I have seen but twice. I don't even know what it says. You would think I should have composed the inscription, but no. Who chose those words now forged in solid metal, permanent, his last and only signifier? And what was I doing when that choice was made? Twitching on a chair in a room in the funeral home as voices buzzed? *His name—the dates. Good. Right. How about "Loving Husband"?* The anniversary of his death slips by every spring like silk.

He would not care whether I visited his niche or not (I tell myself) because he was a scientist and only glancingly devout and did not believe in an afterlife. The first time I asked him where his mommy was—as he watered white iris in the back-yard, and in my sunsuit I rode the plywood rocking horse he made for me—he flicked the spray and said, *She's dead*. Not knowing quite what that meant, I said: *But WHERE is she?* With that caramel almost-laugh of his, he said: *Nowhere. She's dead*.

Yet he observed *yahrzeit* for her: burning the 24-hour votive candle in its chunky glass surrounded by a Hebrew label every year on the anniversary of her death. He recited the Kaddish prayer by which one asks God to forgive the dead one's sins. In temple, he participated in the *yizkor* service, asking God at Yom Kippur to remember her name. He did this for his father, too, although my father never knew his father, who died suddenly and young. My father said the prayers and burned the candles, as my mother did, as their mothers did. And it all ends with me. I do none of it. I do nothing.

Why? How hard would it be to pick up a couple of candles at Safeway once or twice every year? How hard would it be to recite a prayer? I can't read Hebrew, but they spell it out phonetically and provide an English translation in prayer books, in pamphlets, and online—

OK, so I just went to Judaism101.com and did it for the first time in my life. It took two minutes. Not a hard prayer: peace, praise, exaltation. Two minutes is all.

My father was a modern guy. He wore drip-dry trousers and designed satellites. His favorite show was *Laugh-In*. Yet he said Kaddish and lit candles. It was not about religion so much as about doing what was done before. His mother was from a village across the sea. She lit candles although she was forbidden, as an Orthodox female, to say the prayer aloud. A line of her ancestors before her lit candles and said the prayer. Candle on candle, year on year, Jew on Jew: a field of lights, a vast chorus of *yeetgadal v'yeetkadash sh'mey rabbah amen.* All of them, and all those on my mother's side doing the same thing. And then me: obliterator of tradition. Poisoner of troths. Behind this mild smile lurks a destroyer of what went on for centuries: destroyed not on the pretext of some rebellion, not through anger but through sloth. What is the difference between my father and me that broke the chain? I was not taught. He never said, *Learn this. Do this.* Did he assume? Did he give up? I know by heart the prologue to *The Canterbury Tales.* I can recite it but not fifteen little Hebrew lines. The silence falls.

MY FRIEND JUSTIN was a child when his beloved father died. After the funeral, neither Justin nor his mother or sisters ever went to the cemetery. Years went by. They kept devising excuses not to go. Justin grew up. One day he decided to visit. He called the cemetery the day before going, just to make sure, as he puts it, that his father was really there.

The lady on the other end of the phone, in a sweet voice, says: Oh, yes, he's here. . . . He's in our Community Niche.

Justin woke up that next morning *with a sharp pain in my back, between my left shoulder blade and spine . . . as if an intruder had come in during the night, stabbed me with a dagger, twisted it one half-turn, and then knocked off the handle.* He walked to the car hunched over and stiff.

He felt sore throughout the drive—and it was really such a short drive, just an hour or so, though he had always told himself it was far, a whole day's journey. He chided himself for holding onto this misconception always. But how long was always? *And then it came to me: my dad's been dead eighteen years. Eighteen years. Where have I been?*

· · ·

As the youngest of four children growing up in China, my friend Ming was well versed in the Confucian dicta of filial piety and ancestor worship. In the 1960s, politics turned it all upside-down. Ming's well-respected math-teacher father was persuaded to speak his mind against Mao's government, then as part of a national sweep was arrested and sent into exile. Dishonored, divorced by his wife, Ming's father spent the next ten years doing hard labor in the far northern wasteland. A strapping youth, Ming traveled by train to join his father there twice a year. Together they worked the unforgiving soil, subsisting on scant rations that made them ill.

My father and I were very close. I was the only one from my family who visited him, Ming says now. *No one else went out there.* When the exile ended and his father wanted to start teaching again, *I helped him remember his math,* Ming recalls. *He was rusty, but I had learned a lot of calculus and helped him to regain it.*

Father and son remained close when Ming married a girl his family adored. But after Ming and his wife brought their baby son to live in America a few years later, the young couple began fighting and decided to separate. Ming's father was furious. Whenever they talked on the phone, Ming would listen to his father shouting at him, asking what kind of idiot wouldn't want such a nice girl.

Sure, she seemed nice to him. He didn't have to live with her! He had his mind made up. I couldn't win. All he did was complain, complain, complain. Ming telephoned less and less frequently. His father started sending letters. *Five pages, six pages, all about my ex-wife and what was wrong with me.* After a while, Ming stopped opening the letters. *What was the point? I tossed them.* By this time, the old man was living with Ming's eldest sister. The Cultural Revolution notwithstanding, Confucian traditions still held: she looked after him, and all three other siblings sent money monthly to help her from wherever they were.

The old man was hanging a framed calligraphy on the wall when he fell and broke his hip. He died in the hospital, Ming says. *But I never knew that. I never knew anything. I kept calling and calling and no one answered.* It was weeks before another relative told Ming that his father was dead, the cremation and funeral service long over. Ming was appalled. His sister said she hadn't told him because Ming wouldn't have been able to afford a round-trip ticket to China anyway and his visa wasn't completely settled yet and she thought he would have anguished over the dilemma. *So she made this decision for me. She said: what difference does it make that you can't come back and say good-bye to Dad?*

It did make a difference, though. It does.

Ming sees no ancestor worship in his own future. Raised in America, his son is now a university student. He never comes home. He spends his long winter and spring breaks at the houses of friends. He almost never calls.

When Ming dies—whenever that might be—will his son arrive in time for the services? Will he touch the corpse? Choose clothes for it, dress it? Burn incense before it? Ming thinks not.

To what, then, is our wiring connected?

To THIN AIR, often enough. And to a certain monument in Paris. It stands fifteen feet high, with a pronged golden top that resembles a rosebud or a flame. Rising from a tapered pedestal in a small undistinguished square far from the main tourist attractions, the structure is unsightly. Its topknot is asymmetrical, not in a nice way.

When I saw this monument in the autumn of 1998, it was plastered with letters and cards, snapshots, cutout magazine pages, notes scribbled on napkins. A driving rain was making the inscriptions run, and pelting petals off the bouquets flanking the pedestal. You could still read some of the messages, blurry and pale.

Diana & Dodi Together in Heaven!
Princess of Our Hearts for All Time.

The cards and photographs were warped from the weather, their corners curled. Coins glinted on the pedestal—impromptu votives.

Figures knelt touching the monument, reading the messages and placing their own. Others stood around it in the square, clutching umbrellas and hunching their backs against the rain.

The monument stands atop the tunnel in which Diana, Princess of Wales, and her lover were riding in a speeding car when it crashed, killing them, in the summer of 1997. Conveniently, the monument was already in place before their deaths. It had been erected ten years earlier to mark the Statue of Liberty's centennial and Franco-American friendship. The bulbous thing on top is a replica of the torch. But in the wake of Diana's death, many mourners who rushed in those first weeks to the scene of the accident very likely assumed that the monument had been erected for Diana's sake, and marveled at how quickly it had been done. In any case the monument's original purpose was subsumed immediately, perhaps forever. By the time I arrived, a year's worth of devotees had decoupaged it with layer upon layer of their homages, assembled bulwarks of flowers that withered and blew away only to be replaced with bulwarks and further bulwarks.

And I thought, What are you all doing here? It's raining. It's cold. Most of you are obviously tourists, which means that you have traveled all this way at great expense to make public obeisance to a total stranger—not merely a stranger but one who, were you to have approached her when she was alive, would most likely have either run away or set her security guards on you. Many of you aren't even British. You could be doing *anything* right now, but you are doing this. If you must memorialize someone, have you no one of your own to do it for? Wouldn't you rather be indoors having fun?

We no longer publicly mourn our own flesh and blood, our own tribe members and chiefs, yet deep inside, we still yearn to stand in crowds and wail for the loved and lost. The millions of pilgrims who poured into Rome upon the death of Pope John Paul II in 2005 showed this to be true. And this too is why our wiring is now connected to such spots as the grave in a Corpus Christi cemetery of the slain Tejano singer Selena Quintanilla Perez, whose death in 1995 sparked at least six books and a movie—a cemetery to which tour buses have brought countless loads of fans, and a grave transformed into a pilgrimage site flanked with bouquets and ribbons in the singer's favorite color, purple, and handwritten tributes hailing "our Selena" and "our Queen." At the nearby Days Inn where the twenty-three-year-old performer was shot to death by the distraught founder of her fan club, administrators changed the room numbers, hoping to keep the death site from being turned into a shrine as well—but the ploy didn't work, and grieving fans arrived in throngs.

Millions among us mourn total strangers.

For their fans, celebrities are surrogate friends, lovers, sisters, brothers. They are masters, sovereigns, saints, confessors. So close, yet so far. Fans fantasize that multimillion-selling CDs speak to them directly. That the star knows them better than anyone else does. It is a one-sided relationship, sort of like playing with dolls. In daydreams, fans cast themselves as disciples, handmaidens, vassals, and soul mates. All for strangers.

Not all of us mourn stars. But those who do declare allegiance. They revere, without apology or shame. Whatever ceremonies the rest of us dodge for our own flesh and blood, whatever prayers we never learn to say and whatever bouquets we do not buy, whatever epitaphs we do not write—*they* do. Outpourings, candid and impromptu. Driving all night just to be there. You have seen them weeping on TV. They are not faking it, not all of them. In 2004, two dozen years after John Lennon was murdered, fans posted elegies online to mark the ex-Beatle's birthday. *He's singing to me*, one declared. *I look in his eyes. And he looks back at me.* At the same site, another pledged: *To my dearest John Winston Lennon, the most incredible being to ever bless this world. You are my hero, my idle* [sic], *my love.* Another mused: *i cant wait to go see you in heaven.* Another beseeched: *Don't ever forget that I love you more than anything in the world.* Again you have to wonder: Really? More than *anything*? Some of these writers noted that they were never Lennon fans during his lifetime because they weren't born yet.

In their throngs, those who mourn stars feel their grief as part of something larger, something for the ages, something magical and monumental, mortality mixed with majesty.

For that matter, many people mourn their pets. You might say any reverence anywhere is better than no reverence at all, that odes to strangers and beasts are better than sacraments unsaid.

ANOTHER DAY IN Paris, crossing the Père Lachaise cemetery, I saw arrows drawn on headstones with chalk. All the arrows were pointing in the same direction, and some were accompanied by the chalked word JIM. I followed the arrows down the long solemn avenues to Jim Morrison's grave, where an international coterie of young travelers was standing vigil. They were smoking, drinking, lighting incense and candles under a cloudy sky. A youth wearing a woolen hat offered me a flask. Was this the thousandth stranger's grave I had paused—had gone out of my way—to contemplate since my own father died, or the ten thousandth? The lead singer of The Doors died in Paris in 1971, and his modest grave swiftly became a popular pilgrimage site. In 1991, on the twentieth anniversary of Morrison's death, Paris police had to disperse the rowdy crowd in Père Lachaise with tear gas. On the thirtieth anniversary, a security force was hired to control a crowd of some twenty thousand pilgrims—the sound of music and the smell of pot hung in the air.

Leaning against an adjacent grave, that of some plebeian

Yves or Yvette, I wondered whether all these backpackers and hostelers and Eurailers draped over Jim's stone had ever lost any loved ones of their own. Most of them were young, so maybe not. But maybe so. Did the tombs of any unsung grandparents or great-aunts or friends languish ignored far away in Tokyo and Berlin, waiting in vain for visits from boys and girls who would never arrive, who instead traveled miles to be here, in Paris—and not at the Louvre or munching *croques monsieurs* at an outdoor café but amid these cold gray stones and eerily silent paths? Had they never lost anyone they loved; were they that lucky? Was Jim's grave the only grave they knew on earth, or the only one on earth that they wanted to know?

12.

self-absorption

WHEN SOMEONE GOES and leaves us, we are stuck with ourselves. With what is left and with what we are. And what we see makes us so sorry for ourselves. Scariest of all is when we search and search and see nothing at all.

Because, honestly, it's so much to expect of anyone: go on living. *Yeah, right.* Forever means forever. *What?* You're on your own. *You're kidding me!* We all die sometime. *Waaaait a sec.* And now you have to fill the days between today and your final one. *But—how many days is that?*

. . .

Hello?

Hey, I asked you a question.

In the wake of a death, listen—static, phantasms, figments, silence. Look around you: the horizon is forever altered. Even with six and a half billion living souls swarming across it, you can tell. And they say: *Deal with it.* Maybe not in so many words at first. Maybe they coddle you at first. Maybe not enough, from your point of view. Gaze into your eyes and reflected in their shine is the abyss. Others cannot guess what you might do. You might break down. You might explode. They wish you well, they really do, but you are contagious now.

Perhaps you even scare yourself. Sicken yourself. Studies have shown an increased mortality rate among widows and widowers and parents who have lost children. It stands to reason: depressed, vulnerable, drinking and smoking more, insomniac, no longer eating right. Immune systems plummet. Attention wavers from the road ahead. After years of heavy smoking, my friend Justin's father died of a heart attack. Justin's mother, who had quit smoking years before, started again the night he died.

The fear, the fear. The very word *mortality* as it applies not to statistics but to you. The last, worst secret about life.

When a flesh-and-blood relative dies, you cannot help but see it as a preview: someone who looks very much like you, who has your accent and did what you did where you did, someone who was biologically almost you, has been erased. Death has that DNA on file. It has been added to the database. So it begins.

And in that sudden absence, you seem to take up so much more space. But you are not sure what to do with it. This extra space does not feel like a luxury. In its stillness and silence your every gesture feels grotesque, like Baby Huey waddling around in sheet-sized diapers, or like Alice in Wonderland, who after tasting a strange cake felt herself lengthening *like the largest telescope that ever was*, growing so huge that she could no longer see her feet, and wept *gallons of tears, until there was a large pool around her, about four inches deep, and reaching half down the hall*. In your newly emptied landscape, you are enormous, your voice a foghorn. Your pain and fear are encyclopedic, your needs panoramic.

After being married to the novelist Iris Murdoch for forty-three years and nursing her through Alzheimer's in the last five, the literary critic John Bayley called his widowed self "this indistinct creature." He felt desperate "to escape, to evade, to elude whatever was pressed upon me, whether it was telephone calls or chunks of casserole. But I could not escape back into my old self, because my old self no longer existed." Of that vanished entity, "self-pity was the only recognizable trait left over." In his seminal 1917 essay "Mourning and Melancholia," Sigmund Freud explored what happens when we are so identi-fied, so psychologically fused with a loved one as to be left with no sense of self when that loved one dies. This sundered ego—a "narcissistic injury," Freud called it—renders its victims inca-pable of working through grief and returning to their old selves, because they never had actual selves to begin with. Clinging to what feels like the fragment of a soul, the mourner scrambles for traces, making a fetish of the past, dwelling in fantasies.

They call us crazy when we do this. The narrator of Mark Twain's story "The Californian's Tale" meets a middle-aged pioneer who begs him to stay a few days until his wife returns from a trip out of town. *Nineteen her last birthday*, the pioneer gushes, *and that was the day we were married. Ah, just wait till you see her!* The guest stays, but on the appointed Saturday when the young woman is supposed to arrive, a party of grizzled men appears at the door instead. These are the pioneer's friends, and they tell him his wife is en route but delayed. They say they have received a message from her saying that her horse has been lamed. Over the next few hours the guest watches as, under the ministrations of his friends, the pioneer becomes blind drunk. They help him to bed, where he passes out. It is only then that one of them tells the guest that his host's wife has been dead for nineteen years. She died six months after their wedding. *And he lost his mind in consequence?* asks the guest. *Never has been sane an hour since,* the friend replies. *But he only gets bad when that time of year comes round.* Every year, the loyal friends perform this same charade, some years even going so far as to *fix up the house with flowers, and get everything ready for a dance. . . . Lord, she was a darling!*

Following the death of a friend, the French novelist Colette declared it "intolerable" to contemplate "all the hours I must henceforth pass without him. You can see clearly that I'm grieving, because I'm thinking only of myself!"

WHEN SHE WAS crowned in 1837 at age eighteen, Queen Victoria was not stylish, not apparently clever, and not very popular with her subjects. Three years later, she married her cousin Albert and gratefully left the labor of statecraft up to him. For the next twenty years, Victoria relied on Prince Albert's stern brilliance to guide the empire. His sudden death in 1861 utterly derailed her.

She wept for weeks on end behind closed doors, refusing to see anyone but her children and a select few others. Soon even one of these children was cast out of the circle: Victoria shunned her eldest son, Edward, Prince of Wales, claiming that his profligacy had weakened and effectively killed his father.

(In fact, Albert died of typhoid.) Ignoring her queenly duties, Victoria became a recluse for the next two and a half years. During this time, her entire court was ordered to wear black outfits. Victoria herself wore a black crinoline gown. The dress was replaced periodically, but for the next forty years—the rest of her life—she wore no other color or style.

Biographers say she insisted that a photograph of Albert's corpse—taken as the prince lay in state—be hung a foot above the pillow on the unoccupied side of every bed in which she slept. She also ordered that clean nightclothes be laid out for Albert and hot water kept fresh in his washbasin. She wore jewelry crafted from Albert's hair.

My griefs and yours matter little in the world, and if we display too much of them for too long we are called maladjusted. We are derided as completely self-absorbed. For monarchs it is different. No one tells a queen to join a widows' support group at the community center. Victoria's grief set the tone for an entire era and an entire empire. Memorials to Albert were everywhere. Visible symbols of bereavement, such as full mourning dress, posthumous portraits, and jewelry made from the hair of the dead became de rigueur on both sides of the Atlantic.

Yet in the midst of a mourning so deep Victoria bloomed into an extremely influential figure. Never having liked politics, she nevertheless developed in widowhood diplomatic skills admired by allies and rivals alike. It is said that while half-refusing to believe that Albert was really gone—she talked about him in the present tense—Victoria simply did and said what she imagined *he* would have done. She became him.

. . .

MY FRIEND ALEX was the youngest son of a youngest daughter. When his mother died, he was thirty and with his brothers planned a large family funeral. For the subsequent reception, they ordered enough food and drink for a hundred.

The church was packed on the morning of the ceremony. Alex and his brothers sat up front, watching as pink and green glints, refracted through a stained-glass window, danced on the side of the casket. Soft music, their mother's favorite Neil Diamond and Carpenters tunes, sighed from the organ. A few of the guests in the crowded pews prayed silently. Alex was looking over his shoulder to make sure all the flower arrangements were in place when the stillness was shattered by a scream.

In the second row, Alex's aunt Rhonda had leaped to her feet. Her chic black straw hat flew off, pinwheeling to the floor. Shouting her sister's name, Rhonda clawed at herself and stamped the floor, her attractive face flushed and slick with tears.

Juuuulie!

It was a church, Alex shrugs. *You know—great acoustics.*

He and his brothers heaved a collective sigh. *I knew this would happen*, Brendan whispered. *There goes the drama queen.*

Rhonda had always had a spotty relationship with Alex's mother, who was two years her junior. Julie had always been the obedient child, not a Goody Two-shoes but sunny and pliant compared to Rhonda, who was moody and spiky and kept getting expelled from schools. In her hippie years, Rhonda would telephone Julie in the wee hours from everywhere—

Amsterdam, Taos, Rabat—slurring, *Why do Mommy and Daddy love you more?* After marrying Uncle Shel, Rhonda had settled down somewhat. But now she was pushing her way to the end of the pew and clattering on stiletto heels up the aisle to the altar, where she fell to her knees before the casket.

How could you leave me, Juuuuulie!

Alex gritted his teeth.

As the ceremony started, Uncle Shel slipped out of the pew and eased his wife back to her seat, but she wailed throughout. At the cemetery afterward, she waved her arms and shrieked, stopping the recitations in three different places. Each time, Uncle Shel reached out and held her close.

And each time, Alex found himself thinking, *Damn it! We're putting away our mom here and I'm trying to concentrate!*

Moments before it was to be lowered into the grave, Rhonda hurled herself onto the casket and lay with her arms around it, wracked with spasms. The choirmaster and Uncle Shel had to unbend her fingers from around its handles and pull her up bodily. Later still at the reception, Rhonda clung sobbing to guests as they struggled to keep hold of their paper plates.

What will I do without Julie? I lost her too soon!

Alex just hoped his brothers weren't hearing all this. Rhonda had known their mother for nearly sixty years, Alex and his brothers for only forty and less.

He still seethes when he thinks of it. But he knows he can't really blame his aunt.

She was the ne'er-do-well. Without my mom to keep bouncing off of, she finally had to face herself.

. . .

SOMETIMES IN THE wake of a death you run run run to coun-teract the stillness and get busy busy busy to defy the emptiness. Who knows what might be created and what destroyed in this whirl that starts because thinking of anything anything any-thing feels better than thinking about you-know-what. After the death of his lover, the artist Jean Cocteau sat staring into a mirror disconsolately for days, drawing a series of thirty-seven self-portraits. The Mogul emperor Shah Jahan lost his favorite wife, Mumtaz Mahal, in 1631 when she died while giving birth to their fourteenth child. He started building a memorial to her. He built and built. Twenty years later, with much of the royal treasury consumed, he had the Taj Mahal.

The claws of grief can conjure new art in this world: new knowledge, fresh starts even if they feel like betrayal at first, and new life of a kind.

When my father died, I was consumed by fear. I could not wipe the hospital and its sights, smells, and sounds out of my mind. They collected inside me as if I had caught through some supercontagion every illness, every accident, every catastro-phe whose aftereffects I had glimpsed through every open door on every ward. Fear took up all my time. Fear required all my attention. I scanned myself constantly for symptoms and my body happily complied. Every spasm was sclerosis. Every spot was melanoma. I stood in the library, crying while paging through medical books. Standing before bathroom mirrors, feeling for lumps and crying. Sneaking feels in public, in res-taurants. Seeming to find things: a small gasp of shock. Slow to compute a sum in my head: crying because I think it is a stroke, a stroke, a stroke such as got him. Leafing through magazines in clinics' waiting rooms and crying, thinking, *How ironic! Leafing through a magazine called* Life *when I am going to die!* Slipping on slick pavement: envisioning neural degeneration. Crying. Having to pee twice in one hour: thinking of kidney failure, looking up bladder cancer in a book, reading that it is rare and appears chiefly among rubber workers. Still not feeling reassured, and crying. Red eyes in the living room. Crying for me.

A pounding headache and blurred vision. Smiling gently, the optometrist said, *Good news! It's just a migraine!* Not believing him, I went to an MD. Migraine. Nothing worse. Just a migraine.

I could almost see my dad doing what he used to do when I cried: he raised his arms to play an invisible violin, as if making a sound track for a melodrama. If he saw me in those clinics he would say, *You always were so selfish. Thinking only of you.*

Whose death is it, anyway?

I don't know how it happened, but one day I started studying Chinese. All by myself. With books and a cassette. I swear I can't remember where the idea came from. Maybe him. He would have loved to have learned Chinese. Not that he ever said so. Every Sunday night for twenty years he ate Cantonese takeout. He made the improper little jokes—*flied lice!* Yet China fascinated him. He always read about it. His all-time favorite film was *The Good Earth.*

I, too, thought it was impossible to learn Chinese. But heck. It was a season of impossibles, unthinkables, unbearables. His death—impossible. Mom living all alone—impossible. Can I make her feel better? Not this time, sweetheart, that is impossible. Can I go back to last month? Last year? He was sitting on this couch eating a slice of cake made from a mix. Impossible.

In a world where everything is impossible, learning Chinese is no more or less possible than sprouting horns. Or getting out of bed.

English was useless to me anyway. No one was saying anything in it worth hearing. Words and phrases once nice and safe now hurt my ears and throat and ricocheted like playground jokes. Nor did I wish to speak to anyone I knew.

Spend all your time on this. Translate everything you see. Shiver with a tiny thrill as you recognize the characters for "beef" and "fried" on the takeout menu, and comprehend bits of the Mandarin evening news about a fire, an abandoned baby, and a jewel theft. Count forward with each stoplight you pass, then count backward. Forsake everything you did before and ignore everyone. They will call you crazy maybe. They will not recognize you now. But did they ever, really? They cannot follow you here. To your new land of miracles. This land of scars.

13.

judgment

MY MOTHER REFUSED to give my father a real funeral. The kind in a chapel, with guests and a reception afterward—none of that. Nor did she want us to sit shivah, the Jewish mourning period based on the verse in Genesis in which Joseph mourns his father Jacob for a week, in which mourners stay home, barefoot, for seven days with all their mirrors cloaked, receiving guests while refraining from cooking, running errands, studying, shaving, wearing makeup, and experiencing pleasures of a sensual, athletic, or intellectual nature. We wouldn't do it, even though we were Jewish enough to immure Dad at the Jewish memorial park—near the remains of Al Jolson, Eddie Cantor, Jack Benny, Dinah Shore, and Moe from the Three Stooges—wearing a yarmulke and tallith in his casket. We knew what the rules were, but she wouldn't follow them.

She loved Dad, of course, and that was the point.

We sat in the car in the rain the day he died. *We don't have to have a funeral, do we?* she said and shuddered. Jews need to make such decisions quickly, as we do not embalm. She held her head. *We don't, right?*

And, see, I knew what she meant. I knew exactly what she meant. I thought that hardly anyone else in the world would understand what she meant, but I knew.

She did not want to have a funeral, because if we had a funeral, men would come to it and we would look at them and wonder, *Why the hell are YOU alive?*

She did not have to tell me this. I knew.

I mean, his co-workers would come, she said, *wearing blue suits.*

I know.

Rain sluiced over the windshield. The street where we were parked—Dad had driven on that street a million times, on the way to the Chinese take-out place.

Blue suits, she moaned.

I know.

And yes: the very idea of such men, of any men but him, was just unbearable. Their flesh pinkish and warm when his was not, their knees and neck joints flexible, their lashes flicking up and down, their corneas luxuriantly slick. With every nod and step those men would demonstrate an ease which we would perceive as insouciance. They would offer their hands for us to shake as if to say, *Just feel that pulse!* And what would we say then? How could we be expected to control ourselves?

We attended his immurement with my aunt, who was our houseguest, and my husband, and a family friend whose purpose was to drive us there and back, as the rest of us were not up to it. The family friend was female and thus less upsetting than a man. Yet she was alive, which was problematic. She exacerbated this by chattering en route about a cruise she had just taken with her husband. *Jerry got a sunburn!*

The rabbi who said prayers over the casket was a man. That was grueling, his baritone, the suit and tie.

My husband was male, too, of course, but with his loud red shirt and shiny curls, he was exempted on the grounds that he was just a boy.

AND THAT WAS how every live human being came to be perceived not as an individual but as a transparency held against an image of my father. Who was this heat-regulator—this breather—standing around, taking up space? Was he smarter than Dad? Better at fixing things? Was his kindness like liquid caramel, alternating with the bitter tang of rages? It began. A brand-new Inquisition.

Tell me it is wrong to judge, *lest ye be judged*. Say we must not play God. I could not help myself. Death gave me a whole new gold standard.

Look upon whomever—stranger, in-law, friend—and ask him with your eyes: Hey, having fun? Enjoying that dip in the hot tub, are you? My dad would enjoy a dip, too, but he can't *because he's dead!* Have dinner plans, eh? Live it up, live guy!

Yeah yeah, this is anathema. This is the diametric opposite of redemption. The core precept of major religions is that every human life is precious. For the likes of me, in mourning, even to toy with the notion that some lives might be worth more than others could be seen as diabolical. I know. A sin. I know. It sounds like madness, all my scrutiny, my tabulations.

And my quarry walked the world oblivious, unwitting, blithe and unrepentant. But of course they did, because the litigations were confined inside my head. How would they know?

No one is perfect. I am not. My father was not perfect and he would have told you so himself. *I can never remember how to spell words that have double consonants*, he would have told you. *I eat too much candy.* But he was no more imperfect than nearly everyone you pass on the street every day. It seemed to me that he deserved to be alive. Yet he was not. And rapists and dictators and those with death wishes were.

JUDGMENT, IN WHATEVER guise, is human nature. It is not just human nature but animal nature to distinguish good from bad. Call it survival instinct. Every choice we make will either keep us safe or, ultimately, kill us.

THOMAS JEFFERSON MADE a bold claim in the Declaration of Independence: *All men are created equal.* But from a physical or economic standpoint you can point out that we are not created equal at all. Some babies are born blind, some not. Some are born brilliant, some not. Some are born into happy homes, some not. And even if *most* of us are created *mostly* equal, variations among us appear almost the instant we are born. Visitors at a day care center observe that one child is quite obviously combative, another passive, one cooperative, another dazed. It is impossible not to notice, and speculate—assume, conclude. Political correctness keeps us from blurting out such things about each other this way, but it cannot overtake millions of years of evolution. We observe. We see.

In the name of equality and self-esteem, in the name of not casting the first stone, we mince around pretending to believe that we are all the same. But we are not, and we know it, and death rears up and proves it.

DEATH IS KIND of random and kind of unpredictable, but not completely. Certain factors raise the stakes. Smoke, drink, eat donuts by the boxful, spend most of each day prone on the couch, live in a crime zone, have unsafe sex, do illegal drugs, mix with felons, and your chances of living out a full span plummet. This sense of bargaining, of stakes we can control, makes us all the more furious when someone dies who seems to have followed the rules. We like to think we know best. We like to think we know better. We like to think we know *something* that can save us or save those we love or give us some kind of advantage over death.

EVERY DEATH MANDATES a separate equation. No two results are identical. Your tallies reveal more about you than perhaps you want the world to see. When we assess the dead, we are fixing our sights on the world that the dead have left behind them. We have to live here, after all. So it matters to us. And in what condition did each of those who left it leave it? How did that one occupy his or her time?

Day after day, death after death, we force our faces to look blank: the smooth forbearance of statues and Buddhist monks.

Meanwhile, inside, we rage and tell ourselves that so-and-so deserved to die and so-and-so did not. Down that road lies horrific bitterness. I know.

Western philosophy insists that every human life is infinitely precious. That simple superlative should put our minds at rest. But infinity is no longer the vast unknowable abstraction that it was when philosophers and writers of scripture preached on mountaintops. In 1874, the Danish mathematician Georg Cantor published his proof that infinity is a definable set and that not all infinities are of equal size. Before his discoveries, infinity had been almost a taboo subject among mathematicians—seen as a figure of speech rather than a specific mathematical value. However, Cantor considered infinite sets not as merely going on forever but as actual entities, having an actual—although infinite—number of members. By this reasoning, an inch-long line can be divided and subdivided over and over endlessly into an infinite number of ever-smaller partitions and points. The number of subdivisions of a line that went on forever in both directions would be infinite too, but . . . bigger. An entirely different scale of big. And the infinite number of points to be found on a plane is larger than the infinite number to be found on a line. As Cantor deduced—sparking fiery debate among his shocked colleagues—there is infinite and then there is *infinite*.

The philosophical concept of variable infinities is reflected in Western law. A police officer is in most respects an ordinary human being, but the murder of a police officer automatically carries a higher penalty than the murders of bakers and candlestick makers and those of us in most other occupations. The murder of a police officer is legally categorized as "murder with special circumstances," because police officers are charged with protecting the rest of us. Thus in the eyes of the law, the life of one police officer is equal in value to that of hundreds or even thousands of lives—his or her own life, plus all of those that he or she is charged to protect.

The special-circumstances law and similar ones make manifest our shared beliefs, putting into practice calculations on which most of us agree. Like the legal system, the mass media purport to cover deaths in such a way that reflects a consensus: *this* death belongs on page one; *these* belong on page two or seventy-two or do not merit a glance at all. It is a chicken-or-egg situation: Do laws and the media affect our prejudices, or do our prejudices dictate laws and the media? Imagine a perfectly egalitarian utopia, in which the top story in the morning paper was headlined *143,932 People Died Yesterday Worldwide: All Were of Equal Importance.* Would you even bother reading that article?

WITHIN ONE MONTH in the autumn of 2004, newspapers ran stories about two women in the San Francisco area who in some regards seemed very similar: they were only a year apart in age, both were married, and both were the mothers of young children.

On October 11, thirty-five-year-old Jennifer Easterling spent the day cruising the inland waters of San Pablo Bay on a Jet Ski with her husband, Corbin Easterling. At seven o'clock that evening, Corbin called his father-in-law from a cell phone to say that the Jet Ski was disabled far from shore. Jennifer's father would later say that during the call, he could hear his daughter sobbing in the background. Even so, he waited several hours before notifying authorities about the couple's predicament. It seemed to him that this was yet another incident that the emotionally unstable Jennifer was blowing out of proportion.

It was the next morning before his call to authorities sent rescue workers to the Jet Ski. There they found Jennifer dead. Corbin told them that she had complained of severe cold in the water during the night. Then, he said, the couple had fallen asleep together and when he awoke she was no longer breathing.

Several weeks later, autopsy results proved that the death was not accidental. Injuries revealed that a hand had been clasped firmly over Jennifer's mouth while she was held underwater and drowned.

In the month between Jennifer's death and Corbin's arrest on suspicion of murder, newspaper reports described a couple whose relationship had been marked by mutual violence and abuse. Both Corbin and Jennifer sported long arrest records. Corbin had served two prison terms and was arrested at least seven times on charges including public drunkenness, methamphetamine possession, vandalism, and driving under the influence. Jennifer, too, had been arrested seven times on charges including battery of a police officer, child endangerment, possession of drug paraphernalia, driving under the influence, disturbing the peace, and spousal abuse. She was arrested four times for bodily injury to a former boyfriend, the father of her eleven-year-old son. Her year-old daughter with Corbin, Dixie-lee, was in foster care. One week before the Jet Ski trip, she had skipped a court hearing and, ironically, was convicted of two felonies in absentia on the day after she died.

Almost exactly one month later, the thirty-six-year-old best-selling author Iris Chang was discovered in her parked car on a rural San Jose–area roadside, the victim of a self-inflicted gunshot wound to the head.

Over the next few days, articles appeared detailing Chang's career as an award-winning historian and science writer who had published her first book at age twenty-four. Her next was *The Rape of Nanking*, a landmark account of Japanese military atrocities in China. A runaway international best seller in 1997, the book broke new ground on a topic long kept under wraps. Chang became an icon for humanitarian organizations around the world and won numerous honors and awards.

In 2004, she was researching another book about another war-time tragedy, the Bataan death march. She was preparing to interview death-march survivors in August when she suffered an emotional breakdown. Her young son was sent away to live with his grandparents while Chang struggled with severe depression.

Papers around the world ran Chang's photograph. The sleek dark hair, knowing eyes, and full lips poised in a half-smile were so different, yet not so different, from the wild mane, toothy grin, and mirthful squint that characterized Jennifer Easterling's picture, plastered in the papers the previous month. If so many similarities pervaded these two lives that ended violently within such a short time, why then do we respond to each of their stories in an entirely different way?

Both are tragic, of course. But note how the stories were

reported in the press. Reports on Chang adopted an adulatory, mournful tone, with reminiscences from fellow scholars and from survivors of the Nanking massacre asserting that the writer's death was a loss, a blow, a shame, a catastrophe in the world of letters and the field of military history. Asian-American students, it was duly noted, had lost a role model.

Stories on the Easterling case were typical crime reportage. Sordid details sizzled on the page, spotlighting a reckless life ending recklessly. Try as you might, you could not find any mention of Jennifer Easterling having contributed anything to society, having left a legacy from which others might benefit, having cut a profile which even in death others might admire. She had been here for thirty-five years, yet those pages of her curriculum vitae remained blank.

I don't mean to pick on her. Really I don't. It's just that death is a finish not unlike the last chapter of a book or the credits rolling at the end of a film. It is when we realize that nothing more in this story is forthcoming that we can speculate, assess, pronounce. Our status among the living affords us the privilege of reviewing a life, just as critics review books and films.

While both of these women were alive, we might have held back from comparing the two. It would have seemed so harsh. It still does. And for another thing, we never *heard* of Jennifer Easterling before she died. Which tells you something else right there.

THERE IS INFINITE and there is *infinite*. Pound for pound, molecule for molecule, the flesh of one of these women was "worth" no more than that of the other. But they were more than flesh.

We all are, and it is these extras, these intangibles, that shape our tallies. Beyond the baseline created-equal worth of the flesh, we give extra credit to those who put forth knowledge, as Iris Chang did. Extra credit for those who generate new ideas. Extra credit for those who heal and who teach. We give extra credit to those who uphold principles we share. Extra credit to those charged with protecting others. In this regard it seems strange that soldiers are sent out in multitudes to risk their lives, but the presumption is that their lives *and* deaths are necessary to protect entire nations and preserve entire ways of life; we reserve a unique kind of sorrow for soldiers. Only soldiers on *our* side, though: enemy combatants are abstractions, numbers, paramecia. And *they* feel that way about *us*.

In general, we give extra credit to whoever furthers our own sense of well-being, our happiness and safety and moral certitude. In an episode of *The Simpsons*, Bart discovers a comet that is perceived to be hurtling toward the town of Springfield. Fearing an apocalypse, the townspeople flee into Ned Flanders's bomb shelter, which is big enough to accommodate all but one of them. A debate ensues to determine who among them should be kicked out: in other words, sentenced to death.

"OK, OK, let's figure out who should stay," says Krusty the Clown, pulling out a notepad. "Let's see . . . the world of the future will need laughter, so I'm in."

Moe, the bartender, argues that people will always "need somebody to dispense drinks, i.e., me."

The comet is seen whizzing toward Springfield as Reverend Lovejoy declares that the postapocalyptic populace will need "religious enlightenment," which only he can provide. Finally the one ejected is Flanders himself, after Homer points out that as the proprietor of a shop selling accessories for left-handed people, "Flanders is the only useless person here. If anyone dies," Homer asserts, "it should be him."

IN LOSING IRIS Chang, the world lost more than Iris Chang. Her book about Bataan would have opened new doors on history, revealing truths that humanity cannot afford to forget. And who knows where her career might have led her—and us—after that?

It stands to reason that the reckless life of Jennifer Easterling probably would have continued to be reckless. In losing Jennifer Easterling, the world lost . . . Jennifer Easterling.

Am I a horrible person to say this? Am I violating an inviolable social taboo? Maybe, but I am only the messenger. It is not I who reckon the essences of these women, but rather it is society itself that does so. For whatever reasons, we at large treat the dead unequally. Every obituary that appears in the paper has trumped the missing obituary of someone deemed less worthy.

AND I TREAT the living *and* the dead unequally: at least in the privacy of my own head. I used to take landscapes for granted. Who was standing here, and there, and who was loping down that pier eating a corn-dog. Then I joined that club of *us,* the left-behind. And landscapes no longer seemed foreordained. And out of nowhere, invisible weapons sprang into my hands. Gunsights slid into place behind the lenses of my glasses. *Stop it,* I thought—I who had never hurt a fly and never will. I told myself, *I'm glad it's only make-believe* but how glad was I really?

Down Judgment Road are tar-pools of bitterness, Artesian springs of resentment, jungles of rage. No compassion lies along that road. No empathy. Travel down that road a certain distance and you will find yourself armed with imagined artillery, or turned into a basilisk, hatched from some anomalous egg, slithering lizardlike, feeling able to murder with a puff of breath, slay with a glance. Someday maybe you really will become that Buddhist monk and stop judging—*someday*, somehow. And then you will be good and generous. You will be petal-soft, not scaly-hard. But in its first flush, in that dizzy rage when it first dawns on you through the dull nauseous haze of sorrow that some deaths seem wrong and some seem right, judgment is a frail weapon—but it is the only one you have.

But the moment you slam your gavel down, they say it is a sin. Yet why, when it is all inside your head and your appraisals injure no one? There are those who take their judgments literally—Hamlet, in fiction, or in real life Ellie Nesler who, in a California courtroom in 1993, murdered a man who was on trial for molesting her son. "He deserved to die," Nesler said afterwards. "Maybe I'm not God, but I'll tell you what—I'm the closest damn thing to it for all the other little boys." But those are the exceptions to the rule, and Hamlet wound up dead himself on the point of a poison-tipped sword. Nesler went to prison. It is not as if I went out there, eyes still wet from my dad's not-funeral, and *wrought* my fancied justice. It was only feelings, only furtive thoughts. My reproofs were as impotent as reeds. No vindication sprang forth with that gavel sound. My quarry leaped across my path like Bugs Bunny heckling Elmer Fudd. My father was gone. That simple fact. Five years turned into ten, then twelve, and all I kept saying, to everyone, but not aloud, was, *Waaaait a minute, why are you alive?*

I knew that I was just a child shaking her fists as kids do and shouting *Unfair! Unfair!* And ironically I should have known better, since it was *him*, my dad in fact, the very one who started this—my dad himself who said to me a million times, *Who ever told you life was fair?* He said it in a mocking tone you should not use with little girls. And as he said it he would snatch the last Razzle and pop it into his mouth. I told you he was not perfect, and he knew it, too.

14.

mordancy

THE NIGHT OUR classmate Denise died, my friend Renée kept giggling. It was nervous laughter, a breathy puff-puff sound.

Help me, she hissed and pressed her hand over her mouth. *I can't stop hop hop laughing.* The wild look in her eyes asked: *Why?*

SHE DID NOT ask. We did not say. We were not dorks who would start blubbering, *It was the shock that made you laugh! The surprise! It was nerves!*

Nor did we need to come right out and say that, of all the girls on the hall, Denise was such a sad sack. So pitiful that she seemed doomed, in retrospect. If this was going to happen to anyone, if someone was going to slide off a chair and die, of course it would be her. Just her luck. It was almost as if Denise knew it all along, too—the way she hung her head when she walked. The way she frowned while rearranging the little carved animals on her desk, posing them in parade formation, in circles, in standoffs. The way, whenever she smiled, she would shrug and sigh, *Oh well.* And little moments like when she pinned up that poster over her desk of a worm atop an apple. The worm was wearing glasses and a top hat. She looked from the poster to Renée and me and asked in the most wistful voice, almost desperate, *It's perky, don't you think?* In the only snapshot we ever took of her, where her hair hangs lankly to her collar, the corners of her strawberry-glossed lips point down. Through thick glasses those dark eyes squint at the camera with what now looks like prescience. Summoned to the lounge where our resident assistant was going to formally announce the death, Renée and I could hear Denise sigh in our heads: *Oh well.*

Which was hilarious, actually.

OF ALL THE socially unacceptable reactions to death, laughter is the one that makes everyone whip around and scowl at you in disbelief, or with hate. Other reactions are easy to hide under a plain sad face. Other reactions need not meet the public eye. But laughter will not lie. You can no more stanch giggles than a seizure. Laughing during a funeral is the sort of catastrophe compulsives fear. And yet it happens. Sometimes the etiquette surrounding death gets so heavy it seems a parody. A Woody Allen scene speeding toward its punch line—somber glances, dismal music, meaningless condolences, casseroles brought by neighbors who announce sepulchrally, *It's spinach-cheese bake.*

The soul is stubborn that way. Forbid it to laugh and it will disobey on principle, merely to prove it can, merely to prove itself alive. An old trick says: for twenty seconds, think of anything except a zebra. Tell the soul that under these circumstances mirth is totally inappropriate. Tell children that they cannot pee until we get to the motel.

Out of the sparkly smiley world, you plunge into that mourning world for which you were never prepared. No wonder Renée tittered like a lady edging into a cold swimming pool. No wonder, when we reached the student lounge, our resident assistant, Otto, was tittering, too. *Hee hee.* Our world had just been turned inside-out. Midterms and making out with econ majors and shaving your legs one day—then, the next, death. So sudden that it seemed a trick, a joke. Almost everything seems funny when you're that age. And now this. Denise's empty room, her little wooden animals, the notes on her desk for an essay on *The Faerie Queene* that she would never have to finish, her kelly-green and American-cheese-colored acrylic sweaters hanging in the closet—but not her faux-patchwork jeans; she was wearing them when she died. Swinging from a hook, a nylon nightie with ALL-STAR SLEEPING TEAM printed on the front. On a shelf near the window—which she had left open—her toothbrush and toothpaste in a brown vinyl pouch shaped like a dachshund. You almost *had* to laugh.

WHEN MY FRIEND Alex and his brothers were trying to choose an outfit for their mother to wear in her casket, they gathered in her bedroom, drawing items out of her dresser drawers and off the closet rack. Alex pulled a tailored sheath off the rack and draped it over his arm. The dress brought back a flood of memories.

How about this? He shrugged with a sly smile. *At least she can't say she looks fat in it.*

The others whirled on Alex.

Brendan looked awestruck: *How can you be so insensitive?*

What's so funny, Alexander? Steve demanded.

Laugh at or around any aspect of a death and this is what they will call you: insensitive. As if sensitivity were a matter of being allowed only one sensation. As if laughter can mean only one thing: that you are laughing *at* the lost one, ha ha ha. Out of malice, or disrespect, or glee.

Being exposed to death—love or not, grief or not—rather than dull your senses, bares them. The thick crust of your hopes and illusions cracks. You are the new thin skin from which a scab has been removed too soon. You are a cracked tooth. You are an exposed nerve. The slightest touch contorts you. Hot or cold, you writhe. In grief, you appear to be in the normal world, and those who see you from the safety of the normal world assume you are with them, yet you are not.

CRACKING A JOKE or even laughing at one works a different part of your brain than the parts that are frozen by terror, the parts bent on self-destruction when you gaze over the cliff and think you'll fall. Soldiers have always known this: laughing in the face of an adversary works wonders. Sometimes your adversary is death itself. Laughter lifts you out of the depths—if only for an instant.

Holocaust survivors report that, stripped of their loved ones, stripped of every vestige of life as they knew it, they laughed. Jokes sprang to their lips like a force of will. One survivor would later recall chortling as her hair was shorn at Auschwitz. Bald girls around her sobbed, demanding to know what she found so funny. She told them it was the first time in her life that she'd gotten a haircut for free. Moreover, she pointed out that if they had hair to shave off, then they must still have heads, which was a good thing.

Inmates devised puns deriding Hitler and the Nazis. Watching their companions die of hunger, they joked that what the camp really needed was a magnifying glass—because it would at least make their portions *look* larger. The camp latrine was a long concrete bench with some four dozen holes set inches apart with no dividers: a festering source not only of shame but of deadly bacteria. Inmates dubbed it the Auschwitz-Birkenau Coffee Shop. Others gave it a nickname that translates roughly to National Buttocks Radio.

AFTER BEING ROUNDED up with his family in Vienna and deported to the camps, the psychiatrist Viktor Frankl and a fellow Auschwitz inmate, a surgeon, amused each other daily by inventing outrageous stories about their imagined life after liberation. Frankl, who lost his parents, brother, best friend, and new bride in the Holocaust and spent the rest of his life pondering and writing about humankind's search for meaning, later recalled being herded into the notorious camp showers: "The illusions some of us still held were destroyed one by one, and then, quite unexpectedly, most of us were overcome by a grim sense of humor. We knew that we had nothing to lose except our ridiculously naked lives. When the showers started to run, we all tried very hard to make fun, both about ourselves and about each other. After all, real water did flow from the sprays!"

As the Black Plague raged through Florence in 1348, Boccaccio observed that while corpses lay "here, there, and everywhere" and the smell of rotting human flesh pervaded the streets, "more often than not, bereavement was the signal for laughter, and witticism and general jollification." Many Florentines, he noted, "maintained that an infallible way to ward off this appalling evil was to . . . shrug off the whole thing as one enormous joke."

IN OUR OWN private hells, we too laugh at our illusions shearing away. At how panic makes us run in circles like bugs in a jar. At how death is so nonnegotiable that all our standby gambits—thinking, wheedling, begging, bargaining—are for naught. This is why Albrecht Dürer, Hans Holbein the Younger, and other sixteenth-century European artists created *danses macabres*—wry paintings and engravings in which Death takes dapper lords and dainty ladies, abbesses and knights, scholars and supple maidens by the hand, his leering skull heedless of their reluctance to go.

AT HER GRANDFATHER'S funeral, my friend Catrina made herself laugh to keep from crying. She comes from a very stoic family, in which showing emotion in public, even at a funeral, is the ultimate shame. It was not grief over her grandfather's death itself that brought Catrina to the verge of tears that day—*as for my grandfather, I just felt relief at not having to see him piss on the floor anymore and not having to watch Gram boil his underpants to get the stains off*—but it was the spectacle of her beloved grandmother, seated beside her, trembling with the strain of holding her grief inside. And if Gram erupted, the others would follow, and would never forgive themselves for making a public display. *So I looked at the coffin and I pictured a lot of naked bodies writhing around it, having an orgy.*

LAST WEEKEND I went to a rummage sale with some friends from work. Arriving together, we agreed to go our separate ways and meet back at the entrance in an hour. Sixty minutes later we all straggled back with our purchases. One man had a bag of LPs. One couple had a paint-by-numbers Last Supper. Another man carried a stack of art books and another a vintage bowling shirt. I had the heftiest parcel: a large white comforter which the saleslady had rolled up and stuffed into a Hefty bag.

I got a blanket, I said, bouncing the bag. *It was only three bucks but it looks brand-new.* I tugged out a pristine corner to show them. *So new,* I said, *and yet so cheap. Somebody must have died before they got the chance to use it.*

It was funny to me but it also seemed true. Why else would a snowy brand-new comforter wind up at a rummage sale? I feel this way whenever I find never-worn shoes and clothing at thrift stores. Someone bought these or got them as gifts, then death intervened. It seems the only explanation.

The man with the art books—his jaw dropped.

Leave it to you to say something like that!

This friend of mine has appeared naked on TV. A picture of him can be found in at least one coffee-table book of erotic photography. He is pierced and tattooed and wears leather and rides a motorbike and you cannot imagine anything fazing him. But now this blanket thing.

Did it cross a personal line? Was he in mourning?

No and no. He has never lost anyone close. And maybe that was why. Luckily for him, he has spent his life uninterruptedly in the world of the living. Gallows humor amuses only those who have stood very close to a gallows. I started losing acquaintances to death when I was four. This is how death becomes a leitmotif. How it lends a certain tang to everything, to sunshine, to happiness. How it makes new blankets seem suspicious.

After ninth grade, that year when our classmates dropped away in almost medieval numbers—in accidents, from gunshots, from undiagnosed medical conditions—my friend Jeannette acquired a certain look that she wore nearly all the time. An almost-smile, white front teeth showing, pale brows lifted over intelligent eyes challenging: *OK, who's next?* Our sense of humor became bitter. Between gales of laughter we were always saying our new favorite words: *mutilation* and *dismemberment* and *putrefy* and *stab*. At barbecues we compared raw meat to flayed bodies and when we arrived at carnivals or Disneyland we would imagine the scene struck by an A-bomb or a plague.

Charles Dickens, too, had a grisly sense of humor, most likely spawned by frequent early exposure to the sight of suicides and murder victims being fished out of the Thames. As an adult, he would remember being taken time and time again by his teenage nursemaid to watch babies being born. Often as not, the babies were born dead or died almost immediately. Dickens wrote of having visited a home where a multiple birth had resulted in a row of several tiny corpses lined up "side by side, on a clean cloth on a chest of drawers." The scene brought to mind "pigs' feet as they are usually displayed at a neat tripe-shop."

Reading Dickens's description of being "dragged by invisible force into the morgue" in Paris, where he is a frequent visitor and where one day his gaze is glued to a "swollen saturated something in the corner, like a heap of crushed over-ripe figs," you can almost hear him giggle.

IN THE SHOWROOM at the funeral home, my friend Alex and his brothers walked up and down the aisles looking at caskets. A staff member in a black polyester suit led the way, defining the virtues of each model. Some of the caskets were painted white. Some were beige. Some were plain pine. Most were glossy black. Some were lined in flocked contact paper, some in wood paneling and some in quilted satin.

Feel that. See? Stroking the satin, poking its cushions, their guide gestured for the men to do the same. *It's soft.*

Steve and Brendan took sharp breaths and looked as if they were going to cry. Alex laughed.

Quit it, Brendan snapped.

Their guide moved on to the next casket. *This model, as you can see, has the prettiest handles.*

Alex pictured his mother. He pictured her standing there right beside him, asking, since she was allowed to enjoy satin in the grave, then how about a minibar? Alex laughed. His eyes stung. He dug his fingernails into the soft parts of his palms to make them hurt, but his chest heaved and he cackled.

Cut it out, Steve hissed. *What are you, Alexander, some kind of monster? Did you hate Mom or what?* But he couldn't. And he wasn't. And he didn't.

15.

rejoicing

WHEN I WAS fifteen I loved my friend Jeannette so much that other girls said it was sick and my dad said she was a devil who had me under a spell. They were all envious, of course. They could not possibly be expected to understand. Jeannette and I went everywhere together, so we were together that day on the school courtyard when we met Derek. He was doing handsprings on the concrete, making it look easy. Jeannette nudged me, wearing her lit-up look of discovery. *Lookit that guy!* He was not her type—she liked blond husky Teamsters no longer in high school; Derek was dark and feline. When he stopped to rest on a bench and opened a carton of chocolate milk, Jeannette strode up to him in that smiling interrogate-a-stranger way.

So what's your name?

D-E-R-R-I-C-K, like an oil derrick? No?

Where did you learn those acrobatics?

Aren't you scared you'll slip and snap your spine? Would you be paralyzed?

If you got paralyzed, what would you do for fun?

Really? So paralyzed guys can jack off?

Who do you have for civics? Mr. White? Get this. His wife miscarried last summer at Disneyland. No, really, on line for the Matterhorn! It's true, they belong to our church, First Presbyterian!

It was all anthropology to her. But his answers were fast, so Jeannette liked him, and of course he liked her—no, not *that* way. Those two could talk on the phone for hours and hours. He cracked her up because he was stupid but smart—knew all the birth dates of the movie stars but believed that there were once castles and moats and kings and queens and jesters in Los Angeles. Defiantly, he said knights used to joust there "in the old days." Jeannette egged him on, but I told him it was ridiculous. He mimicked my voice, *wee wee wee.*

Because Jeannette was the best friend of both of us, we three spent all our time together. Derek had a car, so on Saturday nights we three drove up to Hollywood to drink coffee and watch transvestite prostitutes. Derek and Jeannette spoke a secret code. They walked down Sunset arm in arm with me trailing behind. Derek would look around at me and try to get Jeannette to laugh. *Roo has feet like boats!* he would say. *Roo has Karen Carpenter bangs! Roo has runs in her stockings! Roo has a mustache!* Those two would riff about movies and cars and then Derek would whirl on his deft feet to look at me, as if just notic-ing for the first time that I was there, and drawl, *I bet you wish you had a boyfriend, Roo.* Sometimes Jeannette would laugh and sometimes she wouldn't. In their secret language she would say *Dthgerthgek, sthgop thgeasthging hthger.* It meant: Derek, stop teasing her. But he would never stop.

All these years later I wonder sometimes if she was trying to get rid of me: to see how much she could let Derek say and do to me before I couldn't take any more and went away. I was not a perfect angel, so maybe she thought I had it coming. Derek liked to begin sentences with, *The reason Roo is still a virgin is* and finish them with whatever popped into his mind. *Because her front teeth are little and brown. Because she listens to KHJ-AM. Because she is frigid. Because if a guy came to her house, her dad would chase him away with a pitchfork.*

In the car, on the freeway, he stroked the gearshift: *Roo, come up front and make friends with this. You might learn something.* He made girly pleasure noises. *Just rub it here. And here, ahhh.*

At the mall: *You never buy anything that's not on half-price sale, Roooo, youuuu cheap Jewwww.*

He liked the rhyme. So did Jeannette, the way it made his lips a muzzle. So he drew it out. *Oooooooo.*

You wonder why I stayed. Because Jeannette was there. You ask was I a masochist. You ask how much in fact *could* she let Derek say and do before I went away, and the answer is every-thing, anything. I would not ever go away, because Jeannette was there. I am still trying to live down those things he said—examining my feet and my teeth, are they OK, well sure but no but sure but are they really? You ask did I have no self-respect?

No, none, but still, did that give him the right?

At a school dance, Derek was capering around to the sound of Elton John and pointing at me, saying, *Sweet sixteen and never been kissed.* I never had. He seized me by the arm and led me to the stairs and said, *This is because I pity you.* He kissed me. Dry and quick, but still. Then he told Jeannette, ha ha ha.

You know the rest. Somewhere between then and twenty years later, Derek died of AIDS-related complications. He died on a July Fourth, as the smell of barbecued hot dogs wafted through our ex-classmate Teresa's window screen and fireworks lit the sky. Jeannette and I learned of his death together, all dressed up. It took a few seconds for me to discern what that tingling was. It was joy.

FEELING HAPPY WHEN you hear of a death, even for an instant, is the ultimate taboo. It's the one that flings you right beyond the pale. Beyond confession. Way beyond conversation. That frisson feels at first like relief, a shivery *ahhh.* Then it turns and shows itself exactly for what it is: By turns ice-cold and hot, fleeting perhaps but unmistakable and totally unacceptable. You think *Wishes come true.* You think *Uh oh.*

Because if speaking ill of the dead is a sin, then how much worse to feel like partying.

Even if only for an instant.

This is your deepest darkest secret. And while you might not dance on a grave actually, you are more than not sad. Leagues and acres more.

And what did the dead one do to deserve it? In the Bayeux Tapestry of your past, what invasion does your stubborn happiness avenge? What insult slashed so wide and deep? They tell us about sticks and stones. They say forgive. Forget. They say to love thine enemy. Didn't you try? The second chances, the thousand ingratiating smiles. How cotton-candy-sweet and soft it would be to forget. If wishes were horses then ladies would ride.

CHARACTERS IN HARDBOILED crime novels are always braying, *I'm glad he's dead!* This is OK because when they say this it is always about a scoundrel. It is a cliché of hardboiled crime novels: *He's better off dead. The world's a better place without him in it.* Fiction is full of jubilations over the deaths of slave drivers and maniac kings and criminals, but in real life it is not politically correct to state that anyone at all would be better off dead. A universal halloo over any death is a thing of the past. When Yasser Arafat died in 2004, articles appeared worldwide citing his Nobel Peace Prize and other honors. Britain's *Guardian* hailed Arafat's *undisputed courage as a guerrilla leader.* A BBC reporter wrote of how seeing the fatally ill Arafat had reduced her to tears. By contrast, the *Boston Globe* columnist Jeff Jacoby called his report on the event "Arafat the Monster." Deriding his colleagues for their effusive praise, Jacoby asserted that Arafat had died too peacefully and not soon enough. *In a better world,* Jacoby wrote, *the PLO chief would have met his end on a gallows, hanged for mass murder much as the Nazi chiefs were hanged at Nuremberg.*

Our private lives have their own wars and sieges and crimes, their own despots and evil stepmothers and Wicked Witches of the West. The mature strategy is to flee such undesirables and surround yourself with those you love. Then, hopefully, when your former tormentor dies, you'll be so far away in miles and mentality that you won't even know about it. But now and then, despite your efforts, it comes rushing back: the rage. The ache. Secrets. My friend Catrina was fifteen when she heard that two of her cousins had been in a car accident. One boy sustained serious head injuries and the other was killed.

And I thought, Whee! She stops herself. *That's terrible, isn't it? Am I terrible? But they were both such bastards.*

THE SMILE IS usually only in your mind, a big wide invisible smile, while what the world sees on your face is your mouth in a straight line (as if in forbearance or shock), your chin set square (as if struggling for composure), eyelids twitching (as if trying not to cry). This is what the world sees, while in your mind you smile.

The gladness warms you through and through. Other reactions might arise in time, to be dealt with later, but at first there is only joy. Like sun after a storm, dawn after dark, clothes after being naked in the cold. You bask. You beam, you dream, you float. You feel a stab of guilt, of shame, for nursing this completely unacceptable sensation. This is the gladness that dare not speak its name.

The dead are gone and thus cannot speak for themselves. They are down—why kick them when they're down? With death they have been dealt the cruelest blow. You hear others around you, who are not glad, say: *She was so brave. He was so young. She will be missed. He worked so hard. A shame! A life cut short! Death is so cruel.*

This is no game of hopscotch you have won, no drinking game or dormitory fight, but something at once eternal and immaterial. What hubris to insert yourself into the picture, thinking you have "won."

But I have, you say with that smile.

Because death is cruel, and life is, too.

LOUIS ARMSTRONG POPULARIZED a song in the 1930s in which a cuckold confronts his rival:

> *There ain't no use to run,*
> *I done brought a gatlin' gun . . .*
> *I'll be glad when you're dead, you rascal you!*

Some incidents, habits, and memories never wash out. They *can't.* You wish they would, because the whole reason you are driven to rejoicing after someone dies is probably that he or she did something awful to you, sometime—and how much better for all of us if it had simply never happened in the first place. Still smarting over a certain professor's refusal to give him a job, many years before, Albert Einstein wrote with bittersweet satisfaction, upon hearing that the old scholar was dead: "Weber's death is a good thing." Some joys hurt. One of my friends was raped repeatedly by her stepbrother for seven years, starting when she was eleven and persisting—sometimes with a cocked rifle at her throat—until she left home at eighteen. My friend's mother refused to believe it was true. *Don't say such things!* Was my friend sad when she heard that her stepbrother had died in jail? *Hell no,* to quote her. Was she glad? *Hell yes.* She thought: in jail, on Saturn, anywhere, so long as that scum isn't breathing. At a local carnival the weekend after learning he was dead, she bought a helium balloon and took it up a hill. It was a smiley-face balloon. She held it high and let it go. And thought: hurrah.

I ONCE HAD a roommate named Tara whose mother had lovers. Before Tara turned eighteen and moved out of the house, sometimes one or another of the men was there when she walked in after school. She would turn around and walk right back out, taking her schoolbooks to the library, because her mother, whose name was Ruth, insisted on privacy when she made love *because*, Tara said, rolling her eyes, *she likes to scream.* Sometimes a lover would call the house at dawn and say, *Get ready for me, baby, Big Billy's on his way.* Ruth would race into Tara's room, tear the blankets off the sleeping girl and yell, *Wake up, get the hell out!* Tara would scramble into some clothes in the dark, walk to school, and wait hours for it to start. If it was cold she warmed herself by pacing back and forth in front of the locked gate. The sun would rise to reveal that she was wearing an inside-out blouse and mismatched shoes.

Sometimes a lover arrived at night, while Tara was doing her homework or watching TV. Ruth would welcome him in and hug him, giving Tara a look over his shoulder while mouthing the words, *Please, Tara, sweetie?* Tara would carry her red sleeping bag out to the back porch, with a book and a flashlight.

Tara was not the rebellious type. She learned to live in a certain way. She could never bring friends home after school, not girls and certainly not boys. She did not know much about other families—her father lived in an ashram in India and did not pay child support, having given his savings to the guru—so Tara studied hard, biding her time.

When it was just the two of them at home together, Ruth liked to discuss her lovers with Tara, what they did and said and which ones she believed were for keeps. *Alvin says I make him feel better than his wife does. Ed is thi-i-i-is big! LeRoy calls me his pet pussy.* A few times Ruth showed up at Tara's school in tears and asked the teacher to let Tara out of class, saying it was a family emergency.

I lost the scarf Bruce gave me, help me look for it!

Rodger says his wife found my panties in his car!

Because she smoked two packs a day, Ruth never felt hungry and sometimes forgot about meals completely. The kitchen had in it only what food Tara bought when Ruth gave her money, but Ruth was always grudging with money for Tara because, as she put it, alluding to Tara's father: *Why should I pay my share if he won't pay his?*

Tara looked for coins in the park. In those days a hot dog at the school cafeteria cost only thirty cents. She never starved.

I never staaaarved, she would drawl when she talked about her former life and I looked shocked. *Why would I let myself starve—am I stupid?* A church in town served cheese and crackers after sermons, and Tara knew where fruit trees grew.

She told me this across our dark room at night. I was shocked. Tara was good and sweet, and cleaned motels to pay for her tuition at accounting school. She called her uniform her *poo-pooniform.* Ruth telephoned Tara a lot because she missed their old chats about her lovers, and when Ruth called, Tara would hold the phone with one hand, muttering *uh-huh* while turning pages in a textbook with the other. Sometimes Ruth called in the middle of the night, right after a lover had left, because she was really happy and really needed to tell someone about it, or because she needed Tara to help her interpret something the lover had said. *He said: "So long." Is that the same as goodbye?*

One day when Ruth called, Tara kept saying, *What? What?* into the phone and let the accounting book slide off her lap onto the floor.

Well, she said when she hung up, with a stunned look. *My mother has cancer.*

It was in her lung. A squamous tumor. She was going in for surgery, and Tara wanted company at the hospital.

A TV was blaring in the room where Ruth sat waiting to be rolled into surgery, wearing a yellow cotton gown, hairnet, and matching bootees.

Sweetie, Ruth said. *I'm so scared.*

We put the lemon in the Ty-D-Bol! sang the TV.

I want a cigarette, said Ruth.

Mommy, the doctor's coming in a sec.

I'm scared. It came out less a voice than a vibration, *scarairairairaired.*

The surgeon had a bit of lettuce clinging to his lip. You always wonder what surgeons are thinking. Their jobs are so portentous and horrible, slashing away at death and second-guessing it as blood spurts out. Surgeons cannot escape the look of death, the feel of death. Hearts stop in their hands. They sew brains.

How are you feeling? he asked Ruth.

Fine. She scowled. *Except that I have only a 25 percent chance of surviving this.*

Mommy, Tara whispered, *think positive.*

Ruth looked at me and I did the weirdest thing. I patted her arm. Its pale hair was surprisingly thick, seen up close. The nurse had given her a Valium to relax and now drool was making wet blossoms on the yellow gown. What was I to her then? Nothing, no one.

When she had been rolled out, we walked down the hall to the waiting room.

I feel—umm—complicated, Tara said.

The hospital, that day, as any day, was full of patients. Some of them were kind and some were generous, and some were furious and some were meek and mild. There were patients in every room and some were bound to die: some soon because nothing could save them, some later because the doctors would help them buy time, some later still because of being healed or cured here. But that day, who knew which ones were which? A hospital is like a battery-powered children's board game, with fifty windows and a tiny light in each and players have to guess which lights will flick off when.

I realized in the waiting room that day how tempting it is to believe that catastrophic illness bestows on all of the ill a certain grace, a kind of sainthood, as if the presence of danger and their unbidden fragility transform them into strange magical creatures poised atop a momentous crevasse. Turning one way, they see death and turning the other, they see life. And whatever they used to be is burned away, smelted in the furnace of fever and terror and roentgen rays. It is human nature to say *get well*. It leaps from our lips like a reflex. But it is not true—the sick are exactly who they were all along, but sick.

What the surgeon found in Ruth was larger and more vivacious than he had expected. Within a year she was dead. Those who heard the news told Tara how sorry they were. And Tara the studious girl, Tara the good and sweet, said *thank you*. Inside her head, she was singing. Sometimes she tried to drown out the song, to no avail. You could see it in the way she walked.

16.

uncertainty

WHILE CARRYING A plate of chicken wings out to the freezer in the garage, my mother fell and broke her leg. She had it fixed with steel pins, went through physical therapy, then came home using a cane. *This place*, she groaned and shook her fist at the garage, its shrouded power tools and crowded shelves. It was four years after my father had died and his brown Mustang still hulked there under the bare bulb that hung from the ceiling on a wire—his handiwork. Buckets, brushes, and cans of paint and varnish waited under his work-table, in the dark. A grinning plastic bumblebee bounced on a spring from the corner of the table to which he had nailed it. Running all the way across the wall were wooden shelves he'd built in 1959, now stuffed with the hoardings of three lives, theirs and mine. Thick skeins of cobweb blurred the colors of the folded beach towels; of the vast Styrofoam-and-red-foil val-entine heart, a party decoration, hanging from the wall facing the car. Webs blunted every angle, drifting like bridal veils past the cupboards stocked with who knew what, because they were locked and no one could find the keys.

It's like an educational filmstrip, I said, *about fire hazards.*

Do something, my mother said.

It's a trackless warren, I said.

My husband tore the first of countless Hefty bags off the roll my father had obligingly stored under his worktable.

My mother went inside. I heard her cane tapping the kitchen floor as she walked toward the TV or the telephone, anywhere but the doorway through which she might see me. Her pain was monumental, an obelisk. She did not want to see this irony pulled from the shelves, crates he had labeled neatly five ten twenty forty years ago trusting that he would open them some-day. She did not want to see his handwriting, his name.

We had to throw away his slack split tennis balls, corroded folding chairs, the paper placemats from a trip through Canada. My husband jumped on crates to crush them flat, hauling full bags and boxes down the driveway.

I thought: *Keep it all*. I thought: *Keep nothing.*

I thought, for the millionth time: *Stop hiding, Dad. Where the fuck are you?*

A steamer trunk held his black earmuffs and winter coats, brought over from New York and packed away in mothballs ever since. Golf clubs gleamed softly in a pale blue vinyl bag. He tried to take up the sport, once. An aquarium. Bags of pink aquarium rocks. He was there. He was not.

The sun sliced the far wall as it used to when he worked out here wearing a white T-shirt and baggy trousers, sawing wood to make a bookcase, make a jewelry box, make a rocking horse. At intervals, the wail of passing bells came from my middle school, four blocks away. The sound made my pulse race. *I'm late. They'll mark me tardy.*

Through my daze filtered other sounds: the whoosh of broken matter and the slide of paper being thrown away.

Motel soaps, boxes full. Inner tubes. Spiral pads filled with the obsolescent engineering notes he took at NYU after the war. The fondue forks my parents bought on their first trip to Europe, during their rapturous childless days.

I moved efficiently but dully, like Gigantor.

We found conchs from a trip twelve years earlier to Florida, still reeking. Cold War–era chemistry sets with samples of uranium, asbestos, leaking jars of mercury. My mother's wedding gown, blockish and stiff; the menu from their wedding: *Fruit Supreme, Roast Poulet.* Templates. Blotters. Bon-Jon Instant Bonsai Kit. Boxes of snapshots he took at fourteen, fifteen, when he was fatherless and teaching himself things: how to photograph his mother and sisters, skaters in the park, flowers in a cheap cut-glass vase. How even to take pictures of himself. Posing on a striped couch. Pretending to sing opera. Wet in a shower, of all things. Eighteen. Nineteen. Twenty, the year the United States entered the war.

Who knew he'd had so many girlfriends back then? He would not meet Mom until 1950. He liked big solid girls. Who was that proud one wrapped in a slippery robe, showing her thighs and the dark crease between her breasts, teeth parted in a smug if rather stupid smile, blurredly but clearly postcoital? Who was that one standing with my aunt?

These girls in his photographs, younger in their swimsuits and ankle-strap shoes than I was, his seed, staring into their eyes fifty years hence.

Sometimes you can see your very chromosomes dissemble. All the lives you might have had, were someone else your mother, race through your head like monorails, all your would-be mothers dressed in nurses' uniforms or crooning over saucepans or gone mad, vouchsafing you a different set of legacies, eyes, paranoias. The girls smiled into the lens, at me, at him. And I thought: *Who the hell are you?* to them, to him.

One box was labeled ARMY.

Inside were stacks of paper money issued in Manila by the occupying Japanese. War photos—soldiers with monkeys, soldiers and palm trees, New Guinea natives rowing boats, Filipinos pushing carts and riding carabaos. And at the bottom of the box, tied with a ribbon, was a stack of letters, typed. He wrote one to his mother nearly every day, and she had saved them all.

Dear Mom, How's my best girl?

He meant his mother, who died before ever seeing me. She was his best girl, at least she was then, at least he said she was.

Here I went thru the pains of learning B'sayan and these people speak Banga-shinan, he wrote, a soldier, a single man, age twenty-three. *Imagine my surprise when they couldn't understand me. I am a failure as a linguist. I think I will study sign language and make my hands work for a while. Now, I wonder how I could ask for* matzah brei?

How sick, I thought, that I just stand here reading these. A casual observer of this boy's life and his war. I wished the years could be a corridor, down which you ran and found abandoned versions of your parents, and yourself, and picked the ones you liked the best.

I'm sure anxious to get that film you said you'd send, he wrote. He loved his mother. He loved his camera. *My shutter finger is nervous in the service for lack of service. Take care of me. Thanks for sending the caramels. They melted and stuck to the prunes and nuts but more are welcome anytime.*

His labored signature was absolutely familiar. His delight in animals and fruit was familiar. His constant jibes.

Here is a little poem which I think you will find adorable:

A woman's whim is ever this:
To snare a man's obliging kiss.
And snaring this, to make him pant
For things that nice girls never grant.

Hey, Mom, I picked a flower from a tree. I thought it very pretty. It almost resembles an orchid. I will send it to you. It was blood red. The censor may not pass it but I will try.

For his mother, who was nearly blind with diabetes—and who had cancer when he left, though no one told him because they did not want to worry him, and who would never see the tropics—he strove to bring alive the jasmine flowers, the coral beaches, the caramel and coffee complexions of his new friends.

He skipped the gorier bits—the corpses—and no doubt the most prurient, but mostly she could see what he saw. And so could I.

I, for whom these warm and lucid missives were not meant.

I, who was long as yet undreamed-of as he sat typing on those hot nights, a member of the Signal Corps, manning a radio.

I, to whom much later he spoke softly about those beauties he saw over there and would seek ever since, the fruit and fleshy crimson blooms and slick seashells: he said he knew during the war that he would always have a garden and live by the shore.

I, to whom he said such things when he could say them to no one else—I, at whom he would sometimes scream, Get the hell out of here! I who was everything. I who was nothing. I, the interceptor of his letters, slasher of his privacy, imposer of my angular uncomprehending self into that soft bond between a boy and his mother who spoke only Yiddish but to whom, not knowing how to write Yiddish—it takes the Hebrew alpha-bet—he wrote in English, knowing she could never understand it, but was too blind to read anyway, so his sisters would trans-late, reading his letters to her aloud and writing letters back to him in her words, translating back again, taking dictation. My three aunts' fingers smoothed this yellow army-issue onionskin, folding each letter back into its envelope not dreaming that the next one to unfold it would be who? A stranger who resembled him yet was washed-out, diluted in comparison. I, who tried to please him and must have, sometimes, statistically speaking, yet what I remember him saying is Get the hell out and Slob and You goddamn pig, his voice rising as if to plead: why are you so stupid, so clumsy, and so disappointing, why and what the fuck and how could God do this to me? And I, his only one, the one and only dividend from who knows how many buckets of, a lifetime's deposits of, what should I call it, seed.

(Except—unless—. You see, one of those photographs he took shortly after the war, long before I was born, showed something strange: tucked in among those of his ankle-strapped and swim-suited mystery dates was one small picture of a dark-haired baby girl in Central Park. She looked like me, but was not me. Above the date that he wrote on the back, one word, a name. But a strange name: his name, but with an a at the end. A feminine version of. The child is who? The child is where? Blinking in startled-awake-from-a-nap astonishment, she has his eye color. And mine. It is the commonest eye color in the world.)

He once told me, on the way to get Chinese takeout, that he wished I had never been born: wished that he had no kids at all. On another night he told me that he wished he had a lot of kids—seven or eight. He made both of these statements in the same like-it-or-lump-it voice, and both meant the same thing: a lot or none, but not only one. Anything but you.

Now, here, throwing away his fondue forks and trying on his soft earmuffs, was I, inadequate to this honor, inadequate, thrusting my clumsy head into his private musings. *Here I am again*, he wrote, *trying to get a message thru to Brooklyn. All I keep getting from the operator is, "Are you sure Brooklyn is in the United States?" That burns me up! Never heard of Brooklyn!*

Who was left alive to laugh at his funny story but I: the golem, scavenging with tanned hands that could be mistaken for his own. I the ridiculous, the infantile; I the befouled of whom he asked when I was twenty-three if I was still a virgin and when I said no he smiled and said *I thought not*, then told me a dirty joke. I, whose beauty at twenty-six he rated *moderate*, making a so-so gesture with his wrist. I, his default inheritor, absorber of a certain bank account but also of his cravings: salt air, half-off sales, smorgasbords, isolation, sweets. It was I, after all, to whom he brought a hollow chocolate rabbit as long as my arm, purchased on sale one Monday after Easter. Its candy eyes peered through the cellophane window of its pink and yellow box. Piped icing made a bow tie, bright pink buttons down a crisscross-icing vest. *I'll just take the head*, Dad said, ducking into the kitchen and emerging with a cleaver. *Just the head*, and expert that he was, craftsman that he was, engineer—who, as a boy who never had a pet and scarcely ever even saw an animal in Brooklyn, wanted one day to become a veterinarian but the war got in the way— marksman that he was, master of the straight line, wielder of blades, draftsman, decapitator, he cleft it with one quick stroke. He took the head in both hands, bit an ear, rolling the chocolate on his tongue. *Go on*, he said. *The rest is yours.*

He used to say, *Other fathers and daughters don't tawk like we tawk.* He did. He said that. He ironed my clothes before I packed them for my honeymoon, as if I were going away to school. He taught me to play badminton and darts, but that was long before, in my Disneyland days. He could fix leather shoes so that you'd never know they had a tear, a scuff, a blot. You wouldn't know. He did these things, methodical, eyeglasses glinting, lips in an attentive rictus, not having to say *Leave me alone* because you knew. It was so obvious. On his deathbed, his face went floppy, loose, *but that was later*, at the end. Here in the garage, before, his brown hands guided the power drill making an antique coin into a pendant, buffed to a bright polestar shine. For me, or not for me. Because he just felt like making a necklace and I happened to be there, or else because he wanted not just to make it but to make it for me. Who knows? He drew up blueprints, poured cement, planted his fleshy gladiolus and flutey crimson hibiscus and silver papyrus that whispered along its leaves. Plywood shelves and tooled-leather purses. *This is called an awl—that's awl, folks!* He made those, and satellites, regardless of me, with me or without me, living out his seventy years plus fourteen days with piston-engine precision, no surprises (though once he gave me a tape recorder as a birthday gift, setting it on the floor beside my bed as I slept, pushing PLAY so that it woke me, saying in his voice, *Today is a different day!*). But his was a life of no surprises of a shocking kind, unless you count flying into rages, which I don't.

Who knew how it would end or when? He never knew, teaching himself in that crowded-with-girls apartment physics, chemistry, the functioning and care of Kodak cameras. How would it end? He did not brood. He used to laugh at me when I asked where the dead went. Now here I was, his own disappointing epilogue trolling *I told you so* in my thin reedy voice, a shambler in his wrack. All this paper and suede and nacre, sweet beautiful wrack: but was I incidental to him? Was I anything? Does he remember me? Why should he? What did I ever do for him, actually *do for* him? Nothing. Everything. It is far too easy to lie. Now here in his garage, where his chemistry set with its vials of lethal substances waited in a pine box that he had made himself, sanded and varnished to a yellow-sateen sheen himself—in his garage among his topcoats and matched luggage sets, his rakes and concrete mix and scrapbooks full of canceled stamps—all his things, waiting for him to flip up the latch and tip open their tops again, wear them in cold weather and carry them again, pour them, add water to them, build a patio with them again, pull them down from the dark and say *oh yeah* and turn their stiff pages again, again, again, the postage of a bygone world from letters he received, from countries that no longer exist, a lifetime of senders he will never see again: his things, waiting for his eyes to greet them again. Eager for his eyes, not fooled by mine, they tell him, *Look at me!* They ask, *Where is he?* But I can offer them nothing, tell them nothing. I ask, too. I, mutineer, marauder, infiltrator, spy.

The boy I met today in the marketplace gave me some Japanese money. I will send you some, Mom! It looks like it came straight from the mint. See if you can buy something with it. I can't get a thing for it here. . . .

The girls at the dance sat there keeping their eyes off the boys. I spotted one but before I could get up the spirit, someone had already asked her. But I knew she was the girl for me. She had high cheekbones lightly tinted and a flat nose. While dancing I tried to strike up a conversation and it was strictly one way. She never would look directly at you when answering and you could see how she suffered when she did look at you. Shy isn't the word. I was a little nervous myself. It has been some time since I have danced and being so close to a female—well!

Once I was warmed up, I must have danced with five more girls. There was one little girl that was fifteen but looked eight. I practically had to push her feet around. She took such small steps.

Another girl was the most modern of all. She wasn't very modest and danced well. Of course, I could eat peanuts off her head if she was a foot taller. She was a big city girl from Manila. There were other girls, mostly short, all modest, with little to say. Only one danced close and you could have drove a jeep between us. She was only sixteen and had an expressionless face.

In answer to your question, no, I won't fall in love with a shiksa.

I passed a large bomb crater near a building. It was fifteen feet across and ten feet deep. The side of the building was destroyed. There were other shell holes about. I saw many trenches where the infantrymen had to dig in while fighting. Otherwise the countryside was undisturbed. The horses, goats, pigs, and caribou graze in the field peacefully. . . .

There is something I want you to understand. You may have the impression that your son is a great hero. He is in the Philippines. He is braving the dangers against the enemy and boiling under the tropic heat. Poor boy! He lives in a tent and eats concentrated food. And a few other things that make me look like a god in everyone's eyes.

Well, you are sadly mistaken. I am nothing but a figure in the Army records, being pushed around till a square peg fits into a round hole. Maybe I am of some use and maybe not. Otherwise I just wait around. The real heroes are at the front dodging bullets and eating and sleeping when they can. No, I don't claim to be or want to be a hero. I stay in the background and enjoy what they fought for. I work little and eat a lot. I do as I please as much as I can and try to imitate a civilian. Sometimes we do them one better. They work for a living. As for traveling, I always wanted to do that. Thus far I have seen things I might never have seen. My burden is comparatively light. In other words, I am enjoying it. Only today I received candy, cigarettes, toothpaste, and razor blades, all at no cost.

I wander in all directions seeing the many different things that are heir to a great metropolis. All over the city, streets and buildings are in shambles.

Mom, do you remember Forsythe and Christopher streets when they tore down the houses before building the park? Whole sections for blocks around are leveled completely. The rubble is piled up and frequently you see the former owners searching the ruins. There are also looters who go on a scavenger hunt thru other people's belongings.

I am looking for a good looted watch cheap.

Grief can get even worse than this. It can get so much worse, and I don't want to know.

Ragged children play about. When a GI passes, they shout, "Hello, Joe." If anyone calls me Joe back in the States, I'll bash his head in. I'm tired of that name. It is getting on my nerves.

Yesterday afternoon I visited the little girl that plays piano. I was going to help her in physics but she didn't want to do homework. Saturday is her vacation! We sat awhile and talked and I don't know how it came about, but she started teaching me to play the piano. I'm more than anxious to learn and this morning I practiced on the piano in the day room. Who knows? Something may come of it. I may learn how to play.

The weather is very lovely today. The sky is clear and there is a slight breeze. I took a shower this noon and feel fine. Chow was pretty good and I received four letters from you. So why shouldn't I be happy?

The letters went on and on. They were not about death at all. They were about life.

HE WENT AWAY. He never goes away.
It stops. It never stops.

sources

Adler, Laure. *Marguerite Duras : A Life.* Chicago: University of Chicago Press, 1998.

Alvarez, A. *Where Did It All Go Right?* New York: William Morrow & Co., 1999.

Ariès, Philippe. *Western Attitudes Toward Death: From the Middle Ages to the Present.* Baltimore: Johns Hopkins University, 1974.

Aristotle. *On the Soul.* Cambridge, Mass.: Harvard University Press, 1975.

Bayley, John. *Widower's House.* New York: W. W. Norton & Co., 2001.

Berton, Justin. "Ashes to Ashes." *San Jose Metro*: June 14, 2001.

Callow, Philip. *Louis: A Life of Robert Louis Stevenson.* Chicago: Ivan R. Dee, 2001.

Collier's staff writers. *Collier's Cyclopedia and Compendium of Profitable Knowledge.* New York: P. F. Collier & Son, 1901.

Conklin, Beth A. *Consuming Grief: Compassionate Cannibalism in an Amazonian Society.* Austin: University of Texas, 2001.

[SOURCES]

Enright, D. J., ed. *The Oxford Book of Death*. Oxford: Oxford University Press, 1987.

Fölsing, Albrecht. *Albert Einstein*. New York: Viking, 1997.

FitzPatrick, Lauren. "Brookfield Zoo gorilla dies at 30." *The Daily Southtown*: December 8, 2004.

Frankl, Viktor. *Man's Search for Meaning*. New York: Pocket Books, 1997.

Goodall, Jane. *Africa in My Blood: An Autobiography in Letters*. New York: Houghton Mifflin, 2000.

Greenblatt, Stephen. *Will in the World*. New York: W. W. Norton & Co., 2004.

Grinstein, Alexander. *The Remarkable Beatrix Potter*. Madison, Wisc.: International Universities Press, 1995.

Harper's staff writers. *Harper's New Monthly Magazine*. New York: Harper & Co., 1856.

Hughes, Langston. *The Big Sea*. New York: Hill and Wang, 1940.

Jacoby, Jeff. "Arafat the Monster." *Boston Globe*: November 11, 2004.

Kaplan, Fred. *Dickens: A Biography*. New York: William Morrow & Co., 1988.

[SOURCES]

Kelly, John. *The Great Mortality: An Intimate History of the Black Death, the Most Devastating Plague of All Time.* New York: HarperCollins, 2005.

Ostrower, Chaya. *Humor as a Defense Mechanism in the Holocaust.* Tel Aviv: Tel Aviv University, 2001.

Richardson, Robert D. Jr. *Emerson: The Mind on Fire.* Berkeley: University of California Press, 1995.

Saint-Exupéry, Antoine de. *Wartime Writings, 1939–1944.* San Diego: Harcourt Brace Jovanovich, 1986.

Seymour, Miranda. *Mary Shelley.* London: John Murray Ltd., 2000.

Stashower, Daniel. *Teller of Tales: The Life of Arthur Conan Doyle.* New York: Henry Holt & Co., 1999.

Taylor, Timothy. *The Buried Soul: How Humans Invented Death.* Boston: Beacon Press, 2002.

Thurman, Judith. *Secrets of the Flesh: A Life of Colette.* New York: Alfred A. Knopf, 1999.